cancerandchrist

Spiritual Exploration Through the Lens of a Cancer Journey

Jason R. Hill

ISBN: 1503263126
ISBN-13: 978-1503263123

For my wife who inspires me, supports me, encourages me, makes me think and brings me peace

INTRODUCTION

On February 22, 2011, I received a call—*the* call—from my ENT doc with the results of a needle biopsy of a growth on my left cheek near my ear. When I realized it was the doctor calling I got a pen and paper and prepared to take notes, as I would at so many doctor visits in the coming years. As she spoke, I wrote at the top of the page, "Cancer," as though I might somehow forget this minor detail. Truth is, I just like to write things down.

So began my cancer journey. I have been open about it and happy to discuss it with anyone interested, but who really wants to talk about cancer? Besides, I would rather write than talk. At my wife's urging I combined my love of writing with my interest in spiritual exploration and launched a blog. My illness is more than incidental to "cancerandchrist," but it is less the topic of the blog than it is the lens. My cancer diagnosis did not begin my spiritual journey, but it generated new ways for me to think about things and new questions in my mind. And I love questions.

Likewise, my self-identification as a Christian is also not incidental and is also a lens. I struggle with many of the traditional beliefs of Christianity, but it is my frame of reference. However, the questions I raise within "cancerandchrist" go well beyond Christian ideas. In fact, I submit they are universal, at least for anyone contemplating spiritual issues.

At the request of a few people, including my oncologist, I have gathered the first two-plus years of blog entries into this volume. The hope is that it will serve to spark the thinking of others on their respective cancer journeys as they work through the spiritual challenges such a journey presents. But I also hope that it is provocative for anyone interested in thinking more deeply—or broadly—about issues of faith, religion and spirituality. One does not have to have cancer to know about struggle, fear and uncertainty. Just like every cancer journey is unique, every life journey is unique—yet we share both the frailty and potential for strength that are part of being human. And if you also share the desire to consider the larger questions that come with that humanity, then you have found a kindred spirit here.

This book contains the largely unedited record of blog entries from September 2012 to November 2014. Other than a few elements that involve the electronic format of a blog, I have left them intact not only to preserve their history but also to avoid second-guessing myself. I wrote what I wrote at a certain point in my spiritual and cancer journeys, and tracking the journey is part of the point. The entries include updates on my condition and treatment at the time of writing, but that is more for context than anything else. The particulars of my specific version of the disease are *not* the point.

You will find no answers here, and you may find some of the questions and ideas challenging. That's good. It means you are thinking about some of the most important elements of human existence. Heady stuff. Better to be thoughtful and intentional about the path you take than to blindly follow the one set before you or select your path based on one or two good or bad experiences. Open the aperture and take it all in. And then keep it open. We learn and grow by making the journey, not by deciding we've already reached the right destination.

Thanks for taking the journey with me. It continues at cancerandchrist.com.

Jason Hill
November 17, 2014

Why Bad Things Happen to Good People (or to me)

September 6, 2012

For the first real post of this blog I might as well get to the heart of the matter (or the lung, as the case may be).

My first chemo treatment this time around was on 8/17, and during my treatment I had both the pleasure and misfortune of sitting next to Ally. It so happened that she and I were the only unaccompanied patients in the treatment room (her son would return later), so she struck up a conversation with me. Ally is 88, a devoted Cardinals fan, a reasonably pleasant conversationalist, a generationally-common-level racist, and a fairly insensitive cancer patient.

Allow me to explain. Ally, as I said, is 88. She very proudly announced to me during our conversation that she had been a smoker for *74 years* without a problem—not even a smoker's cough, which she claims would have prompted her to quit. 74 years, she told me, until two years ago the doctor told her she had lung cancer. "Isn't that irritating?" was her punctuation on the story.

Ally said this with no real prompting, suggesting this may be a standard line for her. Having been through a few chemo treatments now, I can tell you that Ally is something of an anomaly. I have seen the occasional polite conversation between patients, but I haven't actually witnessed much of the "what are you in for?" sort of exchange, a la Charlie Sheen in *Ferris Bueller's Day Off* (the answer, in this case, would, indeed, be "drugs"). But Ally and I had already covered this territory. So when she told me the above she knew I am 41 and have parotid cancer that metastasized to my lungs. (She also made it clear that the chemo treatments she gets every two weeks don't really bother her, but while this corroborates my view on her lack of sensitivity it has less to do with my central point.)

So at that point, when she finally said, "Isn't that irritating?" I had no choice but to respond: "You think it's irritating to you, imagine how irritating it is to me." She went on to lament about how her son wouldn't let her drive, and there is no one else to take her because all of her friends are dead. "Well, you're really old," I said, because apparently her arthritis had loosened her grasp of the obvious.

If you were doing your math (correctly) you realized that Ally started smoking when she was *12 years old*. It is meeting someone like her that can give one a new perspective—and not the good kind. I'd much rather meet a kid with leukemia; not because I like dying kids, but because they exist anyway, and the perspective a dying kid gives you is that you don't really have it so bad. But next to Ally I feel like Job. What have I done to deserve all of this? I never smoked, yet tumors sprouted all over my lungs. I eat well, I exercise, I take care of my family...I'm not perfect by any stretch, but suffice it to say if I were to run for office I would welcome the scrutiny of my life. Yet, the chances of me seeing 88 years old are about the same as Ally winning Miss Congeniality at next year's Miss America Pageant (yes, I get that she has a better shot at Miss Congeniality than at winning the whole thing, but she'd have to win Miss Missouri first, wouldn't she? And Miss Congeniality goes better with my earlier assessment of her character, doesn't it? I'm starting to sound a bit English, aren't I?)

So how does one deal with this seemingly unfair development? More to the point, how does a Christian deal with it? I have no idea. All I can speak to is how I—one specific Christian—deal with it. My approach is simple but not easy. I have become increasingly comfortable with not knowing the answers to difficult theological questions; in fact, it is now to the point where I am ONLY comfortable with not knowing. Whenever I feel like I have a definite answer to anything I have a burning need to immediately reassess. That applies more than ever to this, perhaps the most difficult of questions.

While there is no answer, I believe it's critical for each person to consider the question because it has profound implications for one's concept of God (or god). Look at it this way: first, remove the issue of free will. Even if you can come up with some roundabout way that my or some combination of others' free will led to me getting Stage IV metastatic cancer, I hope you can at least stipulate that there are some things that are just absolutely bad and that could not have been caused by someone's free will. If that is the case--if human involvement didn't create the bad thing--then one of three things has to be true: 1) God caused it to happen; 2) God allowed it to happen; or 3) God was not powerful enough to stop it from happening. I see no way around this. And I'm OK with it.

Here is where I make a fairly radical departure from traditional Christian thinking (well, it's one place). I think historically we have made God into a superhero, a supremely powerful entity with person-like qualities, including a will, a plan and a propensity for selectively intervening in our lives. I submit that God may be more of a presence, not a person. I think God is the source of love and life in the world, and the closer we are able to get to that presence the more human and the more divine we become. But bad shit can still happen to us. When it does, my reaction is not to be angry that God caused it or let it happen. My reaction is to be grateful that God is there, available to me, to give me life and love if I can only find the way that works for me to access it. That can be my family and friends. It can be writing. It can be seeing the world. It can be meditation. It can even be cooking. All of these things work better for me than prayer...but that's the subject of another blog entry, I think.

A friend of mine who is searching spiritually asked me if my cancer experience has changed my faith. My answer was that it hasn't, but when I explained my religious views his response was that I'm not much of a Christian. That is probably true in the traditional sense. If I had been raised Jewish, Muslim, Hindu or whatever, I would likely be that. But no matter where I started I hope I would come to the same place. I'm OK with a God that is not all-powerful, as long as I can feel that God is love and always with me. Although if maybe God could throw a couple of mouth sores or a little nausea Ally's way, I'd be OK with that, too.

The Power of Pray-er

September 19, 2012

It may be appropriate that I'm writing this post from the hospital. You see, I forgot to pray for white blood cells...

I'm actually fine. I just have super low white blood cells right now so they're keeping me as a precaution. But being around a bunch of other cancer patients is getting me thinking about some more big questions. How about these: Why does God decide to intervene on behalf of some people, and why doesn't God seem to respond in other cases? Such are the questions raised by an examination of intercessory prayer.

My life's cancer experience, unfortunately, is not limited to my own illness; to this day I still tend to think of my mother's cancer as more significant to me than my own. This is likely true, in part, because experiences are somewhat defined in our minds by their conclusions (so check back with me when mine's over). We lost my mom. But I think what also contributes is how it affected my feelings about prayer. I won't lie and say I was disciplined enough during Mom's illness to specifically and explicitly pray every day for the elimination of her cancer. I wasn't. But I did think about it every day, and clearly her healing is what I wanted in my heart. I often hear people say it doesn't matter what words you use in your prayers because God knows what's in your heart. So does that count? Or did I let my mother down?

Wait, don't answer that. (Actually, don't "answer" any of these questions—or haven't you figured out the theme of this blog yet?)

I don't want to be overly dramatic here. I am not tormented by this. I had questions and difficulties with the idea of intercessory prayer before Mom got sick. But the experience turned my musings into a deeper form of contemplation and forced me to find a place where my mind could rest (for awhile) peacefully on the topic. And so I did. But more on that later.

Let me frame the question more directly: Can you give prayer credit for a desired result and not blame lack of prayer for the opposite? I know one of the common responses to this is that God answers all prayers, just not always in the way we prefer. Setting aside the country music instances of God knowing what's best for us and thus not granting what we ask, this goes back to the big question about bad things happening. Does God have a cosmic plan that we cannot understand that requires what you perceive as bad to go ahead and happen? Or is there some butterfly effect where if the bad thing you don't want to happen, in fact, does not happen then something worse will happen somewhere in Madagascar? Maybe both. Like many of the questions I'll pose, where you land on these depends on your view of the nature of God.

Of course, the possibility I haven't mentioned is that God truly does select where to intervene based on some evaluation of the prayers received: quantity, quality, intensity, associated candles, creativity, grammar, etc. You're not even going to get a "maybe" out of me on this one. If this ends up being the answer, I'm out. I'll go back to worshiping The Avengers like I did when I was a kid (and for 2+ glorious hours this summer—twice). But if you agree with me on this point—that God doesn't save one person and let another in the same circumstance die simply because more people prayed harder for the former—then I think it's important that we're careful about our language regarding the "power of prayer." Nobody at a funeral says to the family, "Well, I guess you have a little egg on your faces, huh? Maybe next time you'll fill out the prayer request card." But when we stand up and tout the power of prayer for someone's cancer remission or healing or prodigal return home, we have to realize how it sounds to those whose prayers have not been answered in the way they wanted. The implication of claiming the power of prayer can be that the prayers of others are inadequate.

All this can lead us to be uncertain about how to pray. Jesus, of course, offers us an answer through the Lord's Prayer, and I have a hard time arguing with it. I have neither the ability nor the inclination to sufficiently or comprehensively break down the Lord's Prayer, but I think it's noteworthy that there's nothing in it about earthly prosperity (I'm looking at you, Mr. Osteen), physical health (beyond daily bread) or granting wishes of any kind. It does say, "thy will be done," but isn't that more about what we do than what God does? And it does say, "deliver us from evil," but I tend to think of that more as bridging our separation from God than keeping bad things from happening. I think what we have is a beautiful prayer about strengthening our relationship with God and doing things to make this world God's world. That's pretty powerful.

What if the power of prayer is really for the person doing the praying—the "pray-er?" That is where I've come down on this (for now). I think it is about building a relationship with the Divine, the Spirit, the Sacred. And I believe it can be something done prayerfully, not just a spoken prayer. Author and scholar Marcus Borg describes finding a "thin place" where you feel closer to that Spirit--could be a physical place, a meditative state, an activity...just depends on what works for you.

But where does that leave us with intercessory prayer? I am so enthusiastically grateful for all of the prayers lifted up for me, but do I believe that they actually benefit me in some way? You bet I do. No, I don't actually believe that God is a person-like being that hears these prayers and then decides whether to intervene and change my prognosis (although, if God is reading this, God should understand that I am open-minded on this point and not hold this particular belief against me). But the knowledge that so many people care about me and are willing to make efforts on my behalf creates a tangible sense of comfort and peace for me, and I believe that affects me physically. Some would say that prayer affects a person even when that person is unaware of the prayers, and I'm not one to dismiss that. I think it's possible there is a cosmic oneness to us all, and prayer can strengthen connections within that oneness allowing one to feel the prayers even when not consciously aware of them.

But most of all—and I mean this—I am affected by the fact that there are more people out there praying (or people praying more) and building or strengthening their own relationships and connections with their own concepts of God. In doing so, they are also strengthening that oneness that connects all of us. If there is good that can come out of cancer (besides the free snacks at chemo), that has to be part of it.

"Local Prayer Group Blamed for Plant Closing"

September 21, 2012

(I did some research on the issue of prayer and found this news article from a couple years ago...)

Bluetown, Michigan—A local church prayer group is the target of scorn here in the aftermath of the recent shutdown of a large automotive parts plant, previously the town's top employer.

Until its abrupt closing three weeks ago, Wells Automotive employed 230 people in this small town near Flint. Those employees arrived at the non-union plant on February 19 to learn that the plant was closed and that each of them would receive just three weeks' severance.

As many as 12 to 15 of those employed are also members of St. Matthew Church of the Nazarene, which holds a regular Wednesday night prayer group. On the eve of the plant closing, however, the group meeting was canceled.

Hazel Barton, 74, the organizer of the prayer group, maintains that the Wells plant was a consistent recipient of the group's prayers. "We always pray for the Wells plant since our town depends so much on it," says Barton. On the night in question, according to Barton, two of the group's seven members fell ill and were unable to attend.

Barton made the call to cancel the group, citing 78-year-old Millie Samuelson's absence, specifically. "She was in charge of snacks," said Barton.

Among those laid off when the plant closed is Martin Cooper, 49, a long-time member of the St. Matthew congregation. Cooper claims that the failure of the prayer group to meet led directly to the closing of the plant and the loss of so many jobs. "I just got through listening to someone stand up in church and thank the prayer group for the remission of his colon cancer," said Cooper. "A miracle, the guy says. And I'm supposed to think this plant closing is a coincidence? I mean, if not the prayer group, then what? Automotive plants don't just up and close in this country."

Ms. Barton, herself, is unsure of her group's culpability. "The power of prayer has done a lot of good for our town," said Barton. "I've seen babies born to women who thought they would never conceive. I've seen injuries heal faster than any doctor thought possible. And recently we've seen a number of local homes become available at surprisingly affordable prices," she said.

"We're very sorry if we let this one get away from us."

Many like Mr. Cooper are not comforted by Ms. Barton's apology. "She can be sorry all she wants," Cooper said. "That's not going to help me pay my $3,100 monthly mortgage payment."

Ms. Barton expressed optimism going forward as the

prayer group's size has tripled since the plant closing. She claimed that with so many dedicated souls praying to God, the plant may very well re-open by the end of the month.

Hillary Dibble, 28, a former plant worker, is one of the new prayer group attendees. "Sure, I was worried when the plant closed," Dibble said. "But then I came to this group. Do you know they meet right outside this big room with huge stained glass windows and these gorgeous gold-trimmed cloths hanging in front? I wouldn't be surprised if the plant is back open by the time I get back from Hawaii."

Calls to Wells corporate offices were on automated forward to the legal firm of Dorcas & Ruth and were not returned.

(It's come to my attention that not everyone gets that this is a fake news story I wrote. It is. Just having some fun at the expense of those that put a little too much faith in prayer and not enough in personal responsibility. No offense to prayer groups intended. They're actually not the ones being skewered here.)

The Gospel Truthiness

October 6, 2012

I was out weeding around the back patio the other day, and my neighbor came over to talk, having just recently heard about my cancer recurrence (if that's the right term). I gave her the details she wanted, and she started to get a little weepy. But then she said, "But you know where you're going, right?" My honest first reaction was, well, I know Alex (my daughter) has a guitar lesson a little later. Where else am I going? Then she repeated, "You know where you're going. You're a Christian." Ah. That place.

I confirmed for her that I was, in fact, a Christian, but I also felt compelled to say that I didn't think that had a lot to do with "where I'm going." After that, for what I at least think are obvious reasons, I didn't want to pursue the conversation further.

This exchange could take me in a lot of directions within the context of this blog's theme, but where it took me immediately was the bible. It's difficult to have a discussion of Christianity without addressing one's feelings about the bible. So I should start by saying that I believe (not that I know) that the bible is a human product. By this I mean more than it was written by human beings, something to which I think most people would stipulate. I mean that I do not believe that the bible is the divinely inspired Word of God. Here is where most mainstream and/or traditional Christians and I part company.

As I've said before, I am not a biblical scholar. I've been in the church all my life, and I took Disciple I, and that's about as far as it goes. But I've also read a few books on how we view the bible and how we might think about it differently. In particular, a book called *The Blue Parakeet* points out that each one of us, regardless of what we say we believe, picks and chooses what we follow from the bible. We use different rationalizations like, that was a different time or that was the Old Testament and Jesus changed things or Paul was customizing the message for his audience—he didn't really mean women should always be silent in church. We pick and choose. And if we pick and choose, how can the whole thing be the divinely inspired Word? Just the Jesus parts? Which parts are authentic when they are inconsistent?

So where I have landed is that the bible is a collection of human meditations on the nature of God, our relationship with God and characterizations of experiences intended to move people in a certain direction. And I treasure these meditations. I have found the bible to be immensely relatable, especially when I studied it from beginning to end. It felt like a true human story—like my story. But that's how I read it: as a story. I don't think it's history, although it has history in there. I don't think it's the final truth, although there is a great amount of truth in there. And I don't think it's the Word of God, although the word of God is in there.

One of my favorite books is *The Last Temptation of Christ.* Even if you've seen the movie, I highly recommend the book. It was controversial because it depicts Jesus as contemplating coming down from the cross and living a long, happy, married life. Of course, it also shows Jesus as a cross-maker for the Romans at the beginning. The book is not intended to be a retelling of the gospel. It's a meditation on the nature of Christ's humanity and one man trying to come to terms with that. I'm not equating a novel with the bible; I'm just saying that there can be great value in a shared human meditation on Christ, even when not even intended to be wholly historically accurate.

While I find the vast majority of the bible valuable, as a Christian I especially value the gospels as the works that get us as close to the living Jesus as we can get. I am not troubled by the fact that Jesus seems different in different gospels; or that there are only two Christmas stories and they are inconsistent; or that the point in time where Jesus becomes the "Son of God" moves back in time as we progress through the gospels. I'm not even bothered by the fact that these books were likely written too late to have been penned (or scrawled) by the apostles themselves. What bothers me is when we spend our time focusing on these particulars and not on the message of Jesus (as I see it): active and unconditional love and forgiveness of all.

It is too much work (for me) to dissect and defend the historical accuracy of the bible; I mean, I'm not lazy—I'd do the work if I thought it was the way to go. But to me it misses the point. Was there really a flood that covered the entire world? Are we really descended from Adam and Eve? Was Jesus' mother really a virgin (sorry, Catholics)? Did Jesus really arise physically from the dead rather than only spiritually? If you ask me my answer to any of these questions, I'll say, "I don't know, but I don't think so." But then I'll follow it with a question of my own: "Why does it matter?" As always, I can only speak for myself, but whether these and other events in the bible are factually accurate has no effect on my faith. I am a Christian because I believe in the example of Christ's faithfulness until death and the heart of his message (as noted above). I get the paradox here: we only know the message of Christ by reading the bible, so why do I believe those parts? This is critical, though: I didn't say I think the entire bible is bunk. Quite the opposite. What I'm saying is the message and the story are the keys, not the historical details.

Marcus Borg, who I've mentioned before, quotes a Native American storyteller who begins each story with, "I don't know if it happened just this way, but I know that this story is true." If you can get your mind around that with the bible, it may open up a lot of possibilities for you.

This brings us back to my neighbor and "where I'm going." Her implication was that I am saved because I am a Christian, as this is what a tremendously common interpretation of the bible dictates. Even if you don't know the verses, you've heard their implications: Jesus is the one path to salvation. Well, for starters, I think this is a very narrow interpretation of these verses. But it also doesn't matter to me. This is like any other narrow and/or strict biblical interpretation: it makes faith about right belief instead of about action. "Believe this, and you're in." I respect those that believe this way and try to convert others in order to save them; I just don't agree with it. As I've said before, there are many paths to God, and I think our Christian bible offers a wonderful path, but only if I don't get hung up on having to believe this or that one thing. If my faith is about believing the right thing in order to get to "heaven," then where is my responsibility to create the kingdom of heaven here on earth?

So the answer to my neighbor's question is, no, I don't know where I'm going when I die, except that it's to the same place that's available to EVERYONE who embraces the love of God—whether they find it through Jesus or not or whether they even call it "God" or not. As ironic as it may seem, I am not comforted by being a Christian because it assures me of entrance into heaven. I am comforted by being a Christian because it informs how I live my life and connect with other people. It's not better than other religions or spiritual practices, but it works for me. And should my life end prematurely, I am at peace because I have embraced mystery and I am not hung up on whether certain words chosen for a canonical text are precisely true.

I don't know where I'm going...but I am not afraid of going there.

The Meaning of Life

October 21, 2012

I spent a little time recently working on a response to a question from a friend. No, not A question...THE question. He asked me why I think we're here; meaning, what is the purpose of human life? It seemed a fair topic for this blog.

First, I do not think that we're here on earth to earn our way anywhere else, like heaven. Prevenient grace, I think, would argue the same thing: we can't earn salvation, it's simply ours. Of course, we can choose to accept it or not. But in some ways that's beside the point. I don't think our time here is about the afterlife. I think our time here is about our time here.

Let me take my best shot at this. To me the whole meaning of life is to participate in something—to participate in the ongoing creation. I don't think creation is something that happened and stopped, but it's happening all the time. We can let it happen around us, try to destroy it, or we can participate in nurturing it. That means the physical creation as well as the spiritual reality. I think when we show love to other human beings we are creating something consistent with god. When we have fun and pursue our passions, we are creating something. And when we stifle ourselves or mistreat others, we are destroying something, just like the physical destruction of the planet. I don't know what happens to us after we die, but while we're here I think our purpose is to create in whatever way makes the most sense for the individual.

Let me get personal here for a minute, and though it may sound like parting words please understand I'm talking about my life *up to this point*. I've made it no secret to those close to me that I have regrets about certain aspects of my life, and this is why. It's not that I think I've led a bad life. Not at all. I've treated people well, I've loved and been loved, and I've had my share of fun. But where I've fallen short is in nurturing myself. I chose a career path early on and stuck with it; then let financial considerations keep me on that path instead of abandoning it for something about which I am truly passionate. I love to write, for example (surprise). And I feel very passionately about progressive Christian thinking (surprise again). Yet I work in competitive intelligence for IBM, a career and company about which I care but don't truly feel passionate. I know all the rationalizations, and many of them are valid: I help support my wife who does amazing things for kids; I take care of my family and make sure my kids can go to college; I treat people well and set an example within the corporate context. I also know that I've made more than one career decision that has left me with a lower income but a much better quality of life (less travel, fewer hours, work at home). So I'm not trying to characterize myself as some corporate sleazebag whoring himself for money and now feeling guilty. Not at all. But if the point of being here is to participate in creation, then I've spent a lot of years spending a lot of hours each day not doing that.

This is not to demean or diminish anything anyone else does. Many people might have my job and relish it. They would enjoy all the elements of it and feel passionate about it, and, as a result, they would find it fulfilling. That's what I want but do not have. That is what writing makes me feel, but I never had the courage to really pursue it. So in this one aspect of my life I feel deep regret. Unfortunately, it is not a small aspect of my life. I also realize there are so many people who do what work they can in order to survive and don't love their jobs, so I end up sounding like a whiner. But I can only speak for myself and what I feel like I've done or not done with what I've been given.

It's only fair, though, that I mention the many other ways where I feel like I'm participating in creation and have true meaning. I am in love with a woman whose spirit is even more beautiful than her visage. I have two girls who are very different from each other and so enrich my life in very different ways. I have friends beyond what I ever hoped possible for me, and it's become even more clear through this recent experience. And I've already mentioned a number of others--they are those things I described as "thin places" where I feel closest to the Divine. For me that is participating in creation. That's when you might say

I've found my "special purpose." :-) These things have been abundant in my life and are the things that I am actively trying to prioritize in my life now.

So the net, I guess, is that I believe we are here to create a divine kingdom here on earth, and we do that by participating in the ongoing creation. We do that by nurturing ourselves, others and the world; by pursuing passions and even sometimes opening ourselves to pain. We love, we laugh, we give, we strive, we cry... and when we're gone creation is stronger for us having been here. After that, who knows?

The Least of My Problems

November 19, 2012

Let me start this entry that will (spoiler alert) be about "the little things" with a not-so-little thing. This past Thursday I got the results of my latest scan, and the tumors are shrinking even more. The doctor used the word, "fantastic" and said that this is highly unusual response. To be specific, there is almost no visual evidence left of the largest tumors in my lungs. However, as a wise man once said, "let's not start sucking each other's popsicles just yet." We are still in the mode of trying to hold off the growth of these cancer cells, which are still there even if we can't see them. But I will take the good news, and there is always hope of another therapy the longer I draw this thing out.

On to our topic...

One of the things I hear from people (including myself) in their attempts to be encouraging is that one relatively minor side effect/issue or another is "the least of my problems" or some variation of same, including, "if that's the worst thing you have to deal with..." or "in the grand scheme of things that's not too bad..." The implication here is that, "Hey, you're still alive. Don't let the little things get you down." I appreciate the sentiment. But the "little things" can add up. I include the following not as a way of complaining; it's just as a way of illustrating my point and could apply to any cancer patient.

- My fingernails are falling off;
- My eye still doesn't close, and my face gets tired manipulating my cheek to close it;
- My smile does not and never will work, and it makes me self-conscious;
- My anti-nausea medication (or the chemo itself) gives me violent hiccup fits;
- My taste buds are diminished, changed and sometimes encumbered by a filminess in my mouth.

Etc. You get the idea. Taken alone, any one of these nuisances or the others with which I deal would certainly qualify as a "little thing," and I would be happy to cope with it to combat this looming disease. And most of the time, even with the combination of factors I manage just fine. But, to be honest, I have my days when the accumulation of effects and the sense of not feeling like myself becomes...not overwhelming, really...but challenging.

My medical oncologist (I remember when I could just say "my doctor" because I only had one) said that one thing she's noted—somewhat to her surprise—is the frequency with which her patients mention the taste changes as a particularly difficult side effect. I understand it, though. My wife and I recently spent four days of vacation in Paris during a time when my mouth was not optimal for food intake. I did pretty well and enjoyed much of what I ate, but some things were clearly limited, and that made me sad. It may have actually helped with the Camembert cheese, as I thoroughly enjoyed a food that we both agreed smelled like my feet after a ten-mile hike in leather boots. But let's agree the taste thing was a net negative. And it continues to be. The little things matter.

This is where I could turn this on a cliché and say that the moral here is that the little things matter in life, both good and bad. So let my cancer experience be a reminder to us all that we must appreciate the little things. As a writer, however, I am offended by almost nothing so much as cliché. So we will not stop here.

I previously wrote about our purpose here on earth and our call to participate in the ongoing creation. The inference by some may have been that this is all about the "big things" in our lives: major life decisions, career choices, deciding whether or not to commit felonies, etc. I expect I even implied, with my focus on career, that the larger elements of our lives define us. Certainly they do to a great extent, but not completely.

I recently had a friend of mine say something unprompted that caught me off guard and that I found particularly gratifying. First, let me say this is a friend but not a close friend. We see each other a couple times a year in groups and communicate only occasionally. He told me that he thinks of me often (given my condition) and that he's rooting for me. But he went on to say that he has always thought of me as a good person and would trust me to do the right thing in any situation—and that others that know me surely feel the same way. I can hardly think of a higher compliment. I don't think I deserve it, but what it tells me is that some of the things I've done and/or said throughout our period of acquaintance with limited interaction have led him to believe this. We've never been in a life raft together or wrestled with moral questions in a professional context together or jointly considered knocking over a convenience store. It must have been little things.

This is an example. When I've lamented in the past about not considering all the proper career options for myself I've had others tell me you can be a good Christian anywhere, setting a good example and showing care for others. I would broaden this beyond "good Christian," but the point is the same. And I have been fortunate enough to hear from some colleagues and even direct reports that at least some of what I hope to convey in terms of caring for others does come through. To say this is gratifying is gross understatement.

So I am left to conclude that there is tremendous power--over time and sometimes instantaneously--in the "little things" that we do each day, including how we treat others, conduct ourselves and make seemingly minor decisions, especially those that are visible to others. At the same time, we shouldn't get carried away with this. Have you seen the ad where one individual sees another doing something selfless and decides to pay it forward with another small act of kindness, and so on? One of these acts, I recall, is holding the door for a blind person. If you're not doing this anyway, you're a douche. I think we can set the bar a little higher.

In the Gospel According to Matthew, the author has Jesus say that the Son of Man will return someday and say, in talking about having clothed, fed or visited him, that "whatever you did for the least of my brothers and sisters, you did for me." Never mind the disturbing nature of the rest of this passage where the discussion goes to judging the sheep vs. the goats and those that didn't do these things "for the least" will be sent to eternal punishment. Like any good Christian I'm going to pick and choose and use Scripture out of context. I like the idea of doing something for someone else—even (or especially) the "least"—doing something for God. To me that is participating in the ongoing creation.

So I think it's safe to say—hopefully in a way, now, that surpasses cliché—that the little things in life do matter. On the negative side they don't take away from the gravity of my overall situation, nor do they overwhelm me or keep me down for long at all. But they matter and have collective significance. Much more importantly, though, on the (hopefully) positive side, the little things I do and say throughout the course of whatever life path I choose have significance for others. They do not diminish the importance of major life decisions, and they don't make me less sorry for some decisions I've made. But I don't have to be Mother Teresa to have an impact. The little things matter. And, partly as a result of this, so do I. And so do you.

The Story of My Life...and Yours

December 3, 2012

As a reader of fiction and frequent viewer of movies, I am a lover of the art of the story. To me a good story is less about what is happening than why it's happening; so it's really the next layer of story that interests me the most. It's the story of each character. It has been an ongoing joke in my family how much my father hates "The Big Chill" because, as he says, "nothing happens!" Certainly the movie is not plot-driven, but I was always fascinated by each character's individual story, as well as their collective story as a group of former hippies and friends (and Wolverines) figuring out who they are as they approach middle age. The challenge for the novelist or screenwriter is to portray enough about a character so that the reader/viewer gets a good sense of that character's story. Focus too much on a single life detail or personality aspect, and the character becomes one-dimensional. Leave out important details, and the essence of the character is lost.

I make a consistent effort to keep one detail of my life—my cancer—in a corner. I still work full time, take care of the household and essentially do all the things I did before I had cancer (other than go running and eat cheesecake—different reasons). Of course, there are many additional things I do, including doctor appointments, treatments, tests, and a few side effect management techniques. But my approach is to do what is required to manage my disease while not allowing the disease to take over. I refuse to be defined by my cancer. This is one of the reasons losing my hair bothers me so much. I am fortunate to be male in this instance and to be going through this during a time when shaved heads are fairly common. However, those who know me know exactly why my head is hairless, and it is the very first thing they notice when they see me. It is a constant reminder, and while I don't expect people would otherwise forget, I do think it would be less prominent in their minds and therefore less "defining." Even for those who do not know me, my thinning eyebrows and lack of facial hair (even though that's not new) create something of a ghostly countenance that suggests this may not be intentional. My new glasses help, but still. I am obviously not hiding from the illness, but I would rather not present people with such a visible and obvious reminder.

Remember "Terms of Endearment?" How much more did we care about Debra Winger's character because of all that we learned about her as a person prior to and outside of her illness? How much more did we lose it when the kid from the Crunch 'N' Munch ads broke down in her hospital room? She was her volatile relationship with her mother. She was her strained marriage. She was her own infidelity as well as those of her husband. She was her dedicated, if sometimes misguided, love for her children. She was her story, and anyone encountering her after her diagnosis would surely have no understanding of her or how she handled the illness without having some sense of the other elements of her story.

This is true not just of cancer patients but of anyone with a prominent differentiating characteristic. You are the lone person of color in an otherwise all-white community, but that's not who you are. You are extremely overweight, but that's not who you are. You are a convicted felon on parole, but that's not who you are. You have a disability, but that's not who you are...I have cancer, but that's not who I am. No matter how dominating one might perceive a characteristic to be, no one is defined by a single trait, experience, act or challenge. I am my story: mistakes I've made, people I've loved and who have loved me, successes, failures, lucky breaks, choices, trials, passions, beliefs, aspirations. And cancer. The illness, how I respond to it and its implications for my life and the duration thereof add to my story. But they only add to it. They don't rewrite it. No good story is defined by a single detail.

This is actually how I view the bible: as a story. As I've mentioned before, when I took a bible study class that worked its way through the bible from beginning to end it was the first time I was able to see the bible as a story. It is a human story and one to which I could finally relate, having moved back from the trees to see the proverbial forest. There is tremendous richness in the individual stories of both testaments, but to read them without the context of the arc (not ark) of the epic is to lose their fullness and possibly to misinterpret them. We can't understand Jews' views of Jesus without understanding their history as a people. We can't appreciate many of Jesus' words without recognizing them in the words of the prophets. We can't understand Revelation...okay, maybe we just can't understand Revelation, period.

But I think the importance of story to the bible goes beyond context to meaning. There is a common tendency to select verses of the bible to guide oneself or others or to support a point of view. Take slavery (please! ba dum bum). We know the bible has been used in the past to support the practice of slavery. But as a human race we evolved in our understanding of the story of the bible so that we no longer believe such a practice fits within that story's intention for us today. Likewise, many Christians use the bible to argue against homosexuality while selectively ignoring the other commands in Leviticus like stoning disrespectful youth to death and ignoring the fact that Jesus calls us to love all and mentions homosexuality exactly zero times. I believe we are in the process of evolving on this issue, as well, and will eventually see that the story of the bible leads us from separation, violence and intolerance to love, kindness and acceptance. We learn. As Dr. King said, "The arc of the moral universe is long, but it bends toward justice."

I just think we get lost in the details of the bible sometimes, defining Christianity around specific beliefs in specific events or statements. But for me the beauty of Christianity is the story of Jesus in the context of the plight of the Jews through their history; the oppression under the Roman Empire; the inclusive revolution of love he inspired; and his faithfulness until death. The fact that some of the particulars don't line up doesn't really matter, nor does the question of whether he truly healed people instantly or rose bodily from the dead. These are details, and while they are important to ponder they do not define the story. They add to it.

So next time you're flipping through the bible looking for a verse to speak to you, consider the arc of the biblical story. And next time you see me look below my shiny head and past my nearly non-existent eyebrows and into my eyes. Catch a glimpse of my story.

Miracle on My Street?

December 21, 2012

It's Christmas time, so why not talk about miracles? Let me start by saying that after my most recent treatment on 12/6 I am embarking on a treatment break. I have been responding well to the treatments, and so I will be on break until my scans indicate I need to start again. Not exactly miraculous, but it feels good knowing that as I recover from the last treatment I am no longer facing another one right away. Merry Christmas to me. And thanks again to all of you who are sending positive thoughts and prayers in my direction.

I just said that my positive response to treatment, while apparently highly unusual, is not a miracle. But there are those that would suggest that it is. There are those that would say that all of the prayers and the positive thinking have achieved something that goes beyond improbable to rise to the level of a true miracle. Maybe they're right, but I would also reiterate my caution of laying too much credit at the feet of prayer (see my post entitled, "Local Prayer Group Blamed for Plant Closing"). Setting aside, however, the secret of my success, is the success itself a miracle?

Before we address this, it is first worth considering

whether miracles still happen at all. Wait, did you catch that? I said, "still happen." That assumes that they did, at one time, happen. Many of us take that for granted, but should we? The bible is full of miracles, to be sure: people living to be 700 years old, parting the sea, rising from the dead...having babies without fathers. This gets back to a central theme of this blog, and that's the essential nature of the bible. The "point of no return" in biblical criticism is different for different people, but for many it centers on miracles. Tell these people that the miracles in the bible were merely stories made up to make a point or encourage an exiled people or that they were misinterpreted because of a lack of scientific understanding, and the conversation shuts down. No miracles, no religion. Jesus was just a guy who said wonderful things. If he wasn't born of a virgin, didn't heal the sick and didn't physically rise from the dead, then he wasn't extraordinary to the point of divinity. That doesn't fly.

But let's assume for a moment that these sorts of miracles did happen. Are you ever frustrated that they don't happen anymore? Sure, Jesus no longer walks the earth, but miracles didn't only happen in the bible while Jesus was here. Wouldn't it be much easier to be faithful if God spoke to you through a burning bush? Wouldn't you be more inspired if you were temporarily blinded by a light on the road to Damascus, Illinois, and spoken to by the risen Lord? The response I often hear is something like, "I see miracles all the time. You just have to appreciate them." Examples often have to do with natural wonders both big and small, including the most common: the "miracle" of childbirth. This is not the same thing, though. In fact, I would offer that is the exact opposite. Biblical miracles are those occurrences that defy natural law, while we often identify modern miracles as occurring within nature.

Not all of them, though, and this brings me back to my current situation. Sure, maybe an unusually good response to chemotherapy doesn't constitute a miracle, but what if I was cured? There are those healings that still occur that modern medicine cannot explain. Are they miracles? Or have we just not yet figured out why they happened? If we document some of them (thank you, Catholics), will we look hopelessly primitive in 2,000 years?

Allow me to suggest that miracles defined as defying natural law are inherently dangerous. Place too much emphasis on them and you become too disappointed when they do not happen. More importantly, I think one's faith can become too centered on them. Since it's Christmas, let's look at the virgin birth. Is your faith challenged if the virgin birth is challenged? Is it disconcerting to know that virgin birth stories were very common in ancient times as a way of asserting the divinity of someone? If it were as amazing then as it seems to us today, it does seem like all the gospel writers would have included it. But the first readers of the gospels would not have thought very much of such a story other than to know the writer was claiming divinity for Jesus. What would have been amazing to those first readers was the nature of this Jesus for whom divinity was being claimed: humble beginnings, nonviolence, teachings of peace and love, acceptance of all—especially the outcasts. I feel like these are the things that should still captivate us, whether Jesus' mother was a virgin or he raised Lazarus from the dead or he healed the sick or not.

Perhaps there has been only one miracle in history: creation itself. No one knows how all that "is" originally came to be. Even the big bang presupposes something that made that bang. And the resulting creation is so full of beauty and elegance and mind-boggling wonders that it must certainly be viewed as a miracle by any definition. I mean, I believe in evolution and science, but I am overwhelmed at the thought of what set all of that in motion. I do not feel the need for miracles that defy these natural laws when the natural laws themselves are so breathtaking.

So maybe all the miracles in the bible happened, and maybe they did not. But take every one of them out, and, for me, the message and meaning are unchanged. Likewise, as much as I would like a miracle to remove from my lungs what has been described to me as incurable cancer, I do not expect anything to happen that defies natural law. I would just like something we cannot yet explain. But whether that happens or not, the meaning of my life is the same: peace, love and acceptance of all and participation in the ongoing meta-miracle of creation.

I wish you a happy Christmas or whatever holiday you celebrate and a new year filled with wonders and beauty.

Who is I AM?

February 5, 2013

Before we get into the nature of God and all that, let me give you a brief update on my condition. As of the end of 2012 there is no visual evidence on a CT scan of the tumors in my lungs. As a result I have been on a break from treatment since early December. I am slowly regaining strength and stamina, and my taste buds are almost all the way back. Even my hair is returning. I go back for another scan tomorrow (Feb. 5th) and get the results on the 7th. Hopefully it remains clear so I can continue returning to feeling like myself.

Many would agree that it is entirely appropriate to thank God for these scan results. Certainly a little gratitude thrown the Big Guy's (or Gal's) way couldn't hurt. But let's examine it a little more closely. I think that whether or not you believe thanking God in these circumstances goes a long way toward revealing your underlying view of the nature of God.

I am going to confess here that I have stopped saying grace before meals unless the family is all seated together at the dining room table (you would not believe me if I told you how infrequently this occurs). I just struggle with what I want to say. Should I thank God for the food at our table? And, if so, am I saying that I believe God took an active role in making sure our family received its daily sustenance? And if that is true, then how do I reconcile my gratitude with the sorrow I feel for all the families who are going hungry while I eat? Or is it more appropriate to thank God in a more general way, for being the source of all things good in the world? If so, then a prayer of thanks at a meal is as arbitrary as it would be while waiting at a stoplight or after each bowel movement (although if you have ever been on chemotherapy you have likely exclaimed a spontaneous 'hallelujah' on the latter occasion more than once).

The central issue here is whether and when God intervenes in our lives, and I think it goes to the heart of who or what each of us thinks God is.

What images enter your mind when you think of God? Many of us will conjure something vaguely or perhaps even vividly human. It may not be Morgan Freeman, George Burns (dating myself) or Alanis Morissette (is my heresy showing?), but it may be the old man with a white beard floating in the air (thanks, Michelangelo). Or maybe you don't have any physical presence in mind...but do you assign human characteristics to God? Does your God think and feel? Make decisions and choices? Have a sense of humor? Well, sure, you might say. God made humans in God's image, so just as we have all of these qualities in measure well beyond other creatures on earth, so God surely has these qualities in infinite measure. But have you ever considered that humans have, in fact, "made" God in *their* image? (For this precise wording I credit one of the contributors to the "Living the Questions" course I've facilitated, but I cannot remember which one)

Who among us has the capacity to comprehend the infinite? Take just one brief moment to contemplate the vastness of the universe and then tell me that makes perfect sense to you. Tell me you fully grasp a being that is omnipresent and omniscient (we've already addressed omnipotent in previous posts) and not only has always existed but always will exist. Many Christians will tell you this is one of the key reasons God sent Jesus: to put a face on God and help us relate to something beyond our understanding. Perhaps. But would you consider that it may also be that humans have assigned to God many of the qualities mentioned above because they humanize God, thereby facilitating our comprehension? I have heard it said that as soon as you assign words, no matter how eloquent, to God you have diminished God because no human language is close to adequate. How is this not also the case with the assignment of personality characteristics?

Chief among the characteristics which we assign God and which I find troubling is will. We hear about the will of God in circumstances both miraculous and tragic--and nearly everywhere in between. It seems the notion is that anything that happens which we cannot understand must have been God's will. I say this is troubling to me because of what it implies about God: that God is either capricious or unfair...or both. It also troubles me because we place a great deal of stock in the idea of free will, so if God imposes a will upon us it calls into question that very idea of freedom. How can we attribute so much in the world to the free will of humanity while also recognizing in God a will that overrides that freedom whenever God decides it is appropriate? What are the criteria God uses?

There are powerful arguments to be made in the other direction. First, one could argue it is that very cosmic, infinite nature of God which makes God's will incomprehensible. I have stated that God is beyond human understanding, so it stands to "reason" that comprehension of God's will would also elude us—that doesn't mean it does not exist. "God works in mysterious ways," goes the saying. One could also argue that it takes only a brief survey of the wonders of creation to decide that God is an active force in the universe, not a hopeful bystander waiting for things to break God's way.

It will surprise no one who has read any other posting here that I have no answers. Perhaps God is at work in our lives all the time, adjusting and tweaking things to help guide us down the path God prefers for us. Perhaps God just establishes the path and outfits us to travel it but then leaves the navigation entirely to us. Or perhaps God is incapable of a specific will for an individual because such a thing is a human characteristic we assign to God. In this case God may be a powerful force of life and love that is available to all but that will meet many in disadvantaged earthly circumstances—circumstances God is unable to change for us.

No matter where you are in your opinion and understanding of God, I encourage you to think about it. Shine a light on your assumptions and embedded beliefs, contemplate them, and I am convinced it can only further your spiritual journey. As for me, I will be content to thank God for the beauty of creation and the place I hold within it. I choose not to praise God for my response to chemotherapy nor to blame God for the existence of my cancer in the first place. My prayer is simply to draw closer to God in all aspects of my life.

Now if God could just get the Michigan Wolverines back to the Final Four...

To Forgive is Divinely Human

March 6, 2013

It is not my intention with this blog to give the impression that I am winding down my life and mapping out the end game. I am not walking toward the light—I'm still very much in the dark. However, the very premise of the blog implies, if not a unique perspective, at least a less common one. One element of that perspective has to be an intimacy with my mortality. I hope you're OK with that. I am.

My latest scan in early February showed a return of one of the tumors on my lung. It is about 4mm in width, so it's still very small. No treatment yet. We'll check its "progress" the first week of April and see where we are. But suffice it to say my treatment break will likely not be as long as I had anticipated. We are buying time with these treatments, and we made a solid down payment last year. (from here you can choose your own over-extension of the metaphor: the creditors keep calling; I'm trying to put a couple of years on layaway; I'll be back on automatic debit soon; etc.)

When one faces his or her mortality there is a tendency to want to "get right with God." Some argue that there are things you have to do to set things straight. Others say there are certain things you need to believe. But many Christians will tell you that you are "saved" through the prevenient grace of God which exists outside of anything humans can do and freely offers the opportunity to choose God's salvation. And in the same vein (no pun intended), all of your sins are forgiven through the blood of Jesus Christ's sacrifice. So you are saved and forgiven. All you need to do is, deep in your heart, say, "I'm down with that."

It's this notion of forgiveness that is sticking with me this week; it seems to be a theme that has surrounded me in recent days. I first want to address the idea of Jesus as a substitute sacrifice that washes away our sin. This is only one theory of the meaning of Jesus' crucifixion, but it is a dominant one in the church. You current or former churchgoers have likely sung many a hymn and heard many a sermon that talks about the salvific blood of Christ; you might even have been a little creeped out by it at some point. The prevailing idea is that human nature is sinful, and God required a sacrifice. Rather than wipe out humanity God sent Jesus to die, and as a result we are all forgiven of our sins. "To err is human; to forgive, divine."

Let me throw at you an alternate view of the meaning of the crucifixion and see what sticks. Not only did God not require a sacrifice to forgive us our sins, God does not even actively forgive people. The crucifixion was interpreted (and expressed) that way by those familiar with the Jewish tradition of sacrifice, which was based on that people's interpretation and understanding of God at the time. Your sins do not need to be forgiven by a deity. You are a human being with an almost limitless potential for good, even as you make mistakes. The more you deliver on that goodness, the more you exercise your humanity and the more divine you, yourself, become. The meaning of the crucifixion is not Jesus' death but his willingness to remain faithful until that death. It is this example that Jesus set by responding to the worst forms of attack by loving his attackers that is so remarkable, and it is the attempt to follow that example that defines a Christian.

(The preceding message reflects one alternate view of the meaning of Christianity and does not, in whole or in part, represent the views of the vast majority of those identifying with the Christian faith.)

The idea that God does not forgive and has never forgiven sins will be a bridge too far for many, and I understand that. This is not an answer—I don't have any of those. It's another way of looking at Jesus that may open your mind so that you find your own place. But if you'll bear with me, I want to continue down this path of forgiveness.

If God doesn't forgive sins, who does? I do. You do. We forgive one another. We do our very best to follow Christ's example and forgive abundantly as perhaps the greatest demonstration of love one can offer. We do not require divine forgiveness, because the forgiveness of others is the most divine thing humans do. While our nature as (non-sociopathic) humans is to do good, it is also to fall short and sin when we are separated from God. To err truly is human. But each of us wields the capacity to forgive, and in doing so we grow closer to God. To forgive is divine, but it is not beyond the reach of humanity.

My favorite characteristic of forgiveness is its selfishness. You can never do anything more nurturing for yourself or for the ongoing creation than to forgive another human being. I listened to a sermon this weekend where the pastor kept emphasizing the "cost" of forgiveness that one can only pay through the resources God provides. I disagree with this to the point of offense. Forgiveness is often difficult, to be sure. Seemingly impossible sometimes. But its rewards are unmatched, as are the curses of its absence.

I mean, seriously. Have you not heard of makeup sex?

I feel exceedingly fortunate to have surrounded myself with people who neither require much in the way of forgiveness nor have much hesitation in offering it to me. But as I face my mortality I look not to God or the cross for forgiveness but to the life of Christ for the inspiration to be more fully human, including to forgive. The cross I wear around my neck is there to remind me to remain peaceful as the storm surrounds me. And there is no peace without forgiveness.

Easter Experiences

April 8, 2013

The Easter season was kind to me as I enjoyed some leisure time on a tropical beach with my family. Nice. The post-Easter season has been less so. I had another scan and visited my doctor this past week and learned of the return of multiple tumors in my lungs. That is, they returned to visibility by the naked eye on a CT scan. We know they never left. So the treatment break is nearing an end. This is not as hard to take as the initial discovery of the spots in the lungs, but it is difficult. It drives home the fact that—barring any new breakthroughs in treatment options—the remainder of my life will be treatment cycles and treatment breaks.

I need me some Easter.

I do not know what happened on Easter morning in A.D. thirtysomething around Jerusalem at the tomb prepared by Joseph of Arimathaea or in the days and weeks that followed whatever happened there. I don't know if Jesus' body was stolen or if the body was even gone. I don't know if the disciples saw Jesus cooking them breakfast or inviting Thomas to touch his wounds or if they were simply so moved by the loss of their teacher that they had visions of him after his death. I don't even know that the gospel writers did not write their very different accounts of the resurrection in order to foster a legend and claim God for themselves and their cause. In fact, not only do I not *know* these things, but I don't even know what I *believe*.

But there is one thing I do believe: something happened

I was surprised to learn recently that 75% of Americans identify themselves as Christian. This is much higher than I would have thought. But even if the number is a little high, Christianity is clearly in the American majority. Of course, being Christian means many different things to different people, but the fact remains that—even with our separation of church and state—Christianity is part of the establishment. Christianity is "The Man," whether it likes it or not. And this is, of course, not new, going all the way back to when Rome quite ironically adopted Jesus as its own. None of us in the U.S. or Western Europe or most other countries in the world runs any personal risk by declaring an allegiance to Christ. How different was it in the months and years following Jesus' death? The Romans didn't just randomly choose crucifixion as the method of execution. It was meant to send a message. Early followers of "The Way" risked everything to follow Christ and spread his good news to the rest of the world. And they did this not long after—if we are to believe the gospels—frequently failing, misunderstanding and ultimately abandoning Jesus.

Something happened.

I know this strikes at the heart of how many people define Christianity. If Jesus did not rise bodily from the grave, then he was just another smart, compassionate prophet with a good take on life. It means he was not the divine Son of God, part of the Trinity, but simply an extraordinary human being. Maybe. As you might expect, I am not going to assert one view or the other (or the other or the other). And for now I am not even going to ask whether it matters to you. I am only going to say that I believe there was some sort of resurrection experience that first Easter season and that I think we focus too much on the particulars of that experience and not enough on the resurrection experiences that occur still today.

Dominic Crossan makes a great point about the Emmaus story where the Gospel of Luke has two disciples greeted by a stranger as they walk from Jerusalem to Emmaus after Jesus is killed. They speak with this stranger for some time, and though he schools them on prophecy with respect to the Messiah, they do not recognize him. However, once they invite him to dine with them and he breaks the bread, they recognize him as Jesus, and he immediately vanishes. Crossan says that this story is likely an invention, but its point that Jesus is only recognized after being invited in continues to have relevance for us today. He says, "Emmaus never happened. Emmaus always happens." The point is the resurrection experience, not the resurrection itself.

Despite the progression of my illness and the sudden drastic shortening of my life expectancy, what I seek most are resurrection experiences--not resurrection. I'm not talking about appreciating the little things in life. That is also a good thing, as I think I've addressed in another post. I am talking about the transformational experiences that make me see the world I inhabit and my role within it more vividly and with greater optimism and passion. Completing my novel was such an experience for me. It proved to me that there is an alternative arc to the story of my life, and it helped me crystallize my own view of the world. Another: discovering progressive Christian thinking and sharing it with others has enriched me in ways I cannot measure and is a recurring resurrection experience for me. Falling in love with my wife was such an experience and continues to be—like Emmaus, it "always happens." And I look forward to yet another resurrection experience when Trey Burke does NOT call a time out he doesn't have in Monday's national final, and Michigan wins the championship it could not twenty years ago. Go Blue!

No matter what happened on that first Easter, I believe that something happened. And I am inspired to recognize the Easters of my life as they occur. I continue to take what steps I can to push back the finish line of my life. But what I long for are the resurrection experiences that transform it.

Into The Mystic

May 6, 2013

I traveled to NYC this past week to see another oncologist--this one at Memorial Sloan Kettering. I've been keeping him in the loop as another voice in my care, and this visit proved fruitful. He introduced a number of considerations that I can discuss with my doctor at home. However, it also highlighted for me how oncology is as much art as science. We simply do not know very much about who will respond to which therapies. I guess if we did we would be closer to a cure. But for many it remains a process of trial and error, which is fine in "Words with Friends" (although it shouldn't be) but has slightly higher stakes here.

A cancer diagnosis can be a lot of things, but for me "frustrating" is near the top of the list. Cancer takes so much out of your control. One paradoxically good thing about the traditional treatments for cancer is that managing their side effects requires energy and focus. Rather than project forward to the consequences of possible treatment failure I am virtually required to center my attention on what I can control: getting exercise to keep my blood circulating, finding healthy foods that taste OK, ensuring I have and take the medications I need, monitoring my temperature, etc. I feel fear when I consider the prospect of beginning treatment again because I know what is coming. But what of the fear of the uncertain outcome?

Despite surveys that tell us fear of public speaking tops people's lists, I would submit that it is fear of the unknown that is most powerful. Think of the power throughout history of racism, for example. It takes not an expert but simply a rational person to identify fear and ignorance as the cores of racism. The more we as a society and as individuals know about one another, the less racism we see. The same is true of just about any "-ism," with the eradication of homophobia, for some reason, bringing up the caboose of the train to enlightenment. We will get there but only by starting with knowledge.

I think this is what makes religious fundamentalism so enduring despite our exponentially increasing levels of knowledge of science, of religions and cultures other than our own and of the deleterious effects of such fundamentalism in all its forms. The fact is that we, collectively, simply will never know for certain the answers to some of the core questions that divide us religiously and spiritually. I've addressed this before as it relates to the bible in my post "The Gospel Truthiness," but let's look at some broader questions. Just from a Christian perspective: Was Jesus the divine Son of God? Is belief in him as the Son of God the only path to heaven? Is Jesus coming again to judge us? Many will tell you that they know "for a fact" the answers to these questions, but that just is not true. Others will say that is where faith comes in. Ah, faith.

Now we're talking.

Hebrews 11:1 tells us in the KJV that faith is the "substance of things hoped for, the evidence of things not seen." Other translations use "assurance," "conviction," "confidence" or even "certainty." Many accept this definition of faith and wear it as a badge of honor. For all things that cannot be proven, they will tell you, they have faith that withstands any argument. Now, I am not knocking faith. By all means, believe what you believe—just don't tell me that I have to believe the same thing, for that is the root of fundamentalism. But what if you lack the substance, assurance or conviction that Hebrews describes, let alone the certainty? Are you somehow lesser for it?

I like to share a video of Rev. Yvette Flunder (search her name and "I don't know" on YouTube) who talks about the peace that comes with being able to say, "I don't know." One of the worst consequences of certainty is the reaction it produces when the person holding that certainty encounters contrary evidence and/or belief. It can cause crisis, conflict—even violence. Each person reading this blog holds at least slightly and I would wager in many cases significantly different beliefs or views on some of the most central themes of our spiritual existence. Imagine if we could all sit in a circle and share those beliefs out loud, one at a time. As we moved around the circle, who do you suppose would feel the most at peace as each intelligent, thoughtful—and differing—perspective was voiced? Would it be those of us who joined the circle absolutely certain of our views which are now being challenged? Or would it be those of us who ended our own contribution by saying, "That's what I believe right now...but I don't know for sure"?

Some would interpret this as suggesting we should not believe in anything so we can avoid being challenged. Not so. I am simply saying there is peace in embracing mystery. Pray, meditate, study, converse...do whatever works for you to determine what you believe. And share it. Don't be afraid to witness to others. But when you do, be ready to shut your freaking hole and listen. I bet you don't believe all the same things you did 20 years ago (or half your life ago—whatever math works for your age). Why should you think you will believe all the same things next year that you do today? I encourage you to let go of certainty.

Cancer succeeded in wresting any lingering certainty from my grasp. From the first day I have been surrounded by unknowns, including the cell type of my cancer, its origin, the most effective therapies, what side effects to anticipate and, of course, my prognosis. At this point it may seem as though it would give me comfort to fall back on spiritual certainties, but, in fact, the opposite is true. My evolving ability to embrace the unknown in my spiritual life continues to bring me greater peace in accepting the unknowns of my disease. I still struggle, but I feel I am on the right path. In the immortal words of Van Morrison:

And when that fog horn blows, you know I will be coming home
And when that fog horn blows, I want to hear it
I don't have to fear it

I Meant To Do That

June 4, 2013

Chemotherapy can be really distracting.

I'm feeling very well and enjoying feeling well, but the specter of beginning treatment again is ever-present: I expect to begin treatment again in 2-3 weeks. One of the characteristics of chemotherapy that seems to span the blessing/curse spectrum is that it sucks enough that it keeps one's attention off the greater issue at hand; i.e., the reason one is taking chemotherapy in the first place.

Let me be clear: it does not slip my mind that I have cancer or that its stage and metastatic nature are less than encouraging. However, since I was diagnosed I have attempted to keep the disease in its place. I have continued to work, to travel, to attend to household duties, to exercise, etc. By compartmentalizing my life I can attend to the disease and then set it aside until it requires my attention again. Even while I am undergoing treatment I try to adjust accordingly and do the compartmentalizing on a daily basis. Take the pill, give myself the shot, apply the lotion...okay, I'll stop there and leave something to the imagination. But then I move on to the next (hopefully unrelated) thing in my day.

Right now, though, the anticipation of treatment is more invasive mentally than treatment itself, and I find it frustrating in the same way I am frustrated when I fail to compartmentalize effectively (and I frequently fail). Somehow the distraction of pending treatment is causing my mind to race no matter what I'm doing. My desire to "live for today" can become overwhelming as I question whether I am succeeding at doing so. I can't concentrate at work because I wonder whether this is the right job for me. I can't concentrate on reading because I feel like I should be writing. I don't fully enjoy a vacation because I wonder if it is the right vacation to be taking. I fail to fully experience anything because I am continually second-guessing whether it's the right experience. It can be almost paralyzing (and I have some experience with paralysis).

Much of this is simply my personality: I have a productivity neurosis. I HATE to feel as though I have wasted any time, and that was true before I got sick. That doesn't mean I don't enjoy leisure time or that there are no tasks in our house that need attention. Quite the contrary. I value leisure time greatly, but it must be scheduled or at least I must have made a decision to experience it. And I can put off household projects with the best of them, but it's because there are other productive pursuits that take precedence. I sound like fun, don't I?

My wife calls this "mindfulness"—or a lack thereof, in my case. I think of it as presence. Thoreau called it "living deliberately." (We recently watched "Dead Poets' Society" with my youngest daughter, who was seeing it for the first time; almost makes me wish I had more kids so I could introduce them to it, as well. Almost.) I am not exactly "sucking out all the marrow of life" when I am constantly wondering whether I should be doing something else. This is one reason I enjoy cooking so much: because it requires my undivided attention (if I'm doing anything daring at all). It's also one reason I'm not a better golfer.

The one area of my life where I feel like I have become mindful, present and deliberate is my spirituality. This predates my illness, though it has since become more acute. When I am reading about faith or listening to a speaker or discussing religious ideas in a group or writing this blog, I am present. I am thinking of nothing else. Yet this remains a realm that many of us neglect. If we are actively religious we may feel as though we have begun doing things by rote without examining our beliefs to take a temperature check. If we are "spiritual but not religious" we may let that phrase define us without exploring and identifying our spiritual needs and beliefs. Our disillusionment with organized religion becomes the end of our spiritual story. And many of us have a sense of a greater reality beyond ourselves but have ignored that nagging sense to the point where we barely notice it anymore.

So I challenge you. I challenge each one of you

reading this to be intentional in your spiritual development. My church has even adopted from our bishop the phrase "Intentional Faith Development" as one of its pillars, but many of us have not really internalized it. If you are not part of a faith community it can be even more difficult. And if you do not identify with a religion or feel alienated by all things God it may feel impossible or useless. So I suggest taking a small step. You've taken one by reading this blog. Perhaps now you should share it with someone and then engage in a discussion on one of the topics. For others it may mean reading a book—I can suggest a few and would welcome suggestions from you. For some it may mean going to church and for some churchgoers it may mean going to a class at church or elsewhere. For some it may mean engaging in prayer more frequently or differently. And for some it may simply mean finding something to do in a prayerful manner, like meditating, gardening, running, volunteering—whatever; just be intentional about it and be present.

This is not a recruitment exercise. If you've been reading this blog all along you should know by now I have no interest in converting people to Christianity or bringing someone to the church unless that happens to be the right path for that individual. Rather, this is simply a call for you to nurture your spirituality in whatever form it takes, with whatever religion it involves or with no religious attachment at all. You don't have to call it "faith." It doesn't have to be about belief at all, and it certainly doesn't need a name. I think it's about relationship, and for me it's relationship with the Divine—the spiritual force in the world that touches us all and connects us all. For you it may be something different. But I cannot imagine a more rewarding way to spend some time than to deliberately, mindfully explore what spirituality means to you.

Carpe diem.

Biblical Proportion

June 24, 2013

It seems that from a number of different directions lately I have been invited to look at things in a new way. I have not yet resorted to standing on my desk, but I'm getting there. (That is "Dead Poets' Society" reference #2 on this blog--I can't promise there won't be more.)

For one thing I am taking a class on thinking using models. One of the examples they used also turned up in a novel I just finished. Perhaps you've heard of it: The Monty Hall Problem. Permit me a brief explanation: You are playing "Let's Make a Deal," and you choose door #1 out of three to get the prize. Host Monty Hall, knowing behind which door the good prize lies, selects door #3 to reveal a goat to you. Assuming you don't want the goat instead of the $10,000 or whatever, you are asked to either stick with door #1 or switch to door #2. Here is where thinking about things differently comes in. Intuition might tell you that it doesn't matter; you have a 50/50 chance because there are two doors left and one of them has the prize. In fact, the prize is twice as likely to be behind door #2, so you should switch your choice. I won't bore you with the probability explanation (you can look it up), but I thought it was cool that this made me think about things very differently.

Speaking of famous Montys, Trish (my wife) and I recently attended the season-opening night of The Muny, St. Louis's outdoor musical amphitheatre. One of the things I've decided over the past couple of years to do is to set aside more time for things I really enjoy. Live theater is one of those things, so we got season tickets this year. Anyway, I say "Monty" because the show was "Spamalot." After the curtain call the cast surprised the audience by bringing out Eric Idle, formerly of Monty Python and the creator of "Spamalot." He said that we were attending the first performance of the show in the open air and that it was the largest audience ever to see the show. Having recently had a few other unique St. Louis experiences I left The Muny that night with a greater appreciation of where I live.

One would think that my cancer diagnosis would have caused me to see all sorts of things in a new light, but I can't say that this is the case. In particular, I had a friend ask me if my faith had been shaken by the diagnosis or if I saw God differently. The honest answer was no. I had been questioning traditional Christian thinking and intentionally working through my feelings about religion for some time. I actually think this has made dealing with the disease easier for me than it would have been if my beliefs had been more rigid. However, getting cancer may have accelerated and intensified my questioning in some areas, and one of those is the Bible. I've addressed views of the Bible before in a previous post, but I feel moved to do so again. I've also been reading a book Trish got me for Father's Day: *Reading the Bible Again for the First Time* by Marcus Borg. It raises a number of points I've heard before from him and others, but, again, it's useful to take another look.

Let me first say I think the Bible is worth another look--a different look--no matter what your current relationship is with it. If you believe the Bible is the divine Word of God and can recite whole passages from memory, I think there is another way of viewing it that you might find insightful--even liberating. If you feel the Bible has no relevance to your life and have spent little or no time paying any attention to it at all, I encourage you to stick with me here. I think there is a way into the Bible for you, and you may end up finding it life-affirming and relatable. Most of you are somewhere in between, so if it is worthwhile for the extremes then I think you will find it worthwhile for you.

The different look I am proposing is this: consider the Bible as the work of the people of ancient Israel and the early Christian movement as they wrestled with their experiences with and understanding of God. In other words, try looking at the Bible as the meditations of a specific set of human beings at a specific point in history. I won't get into here the discussion of literal vs. metaphor vs. storytelling; the idea I'm suggesting is related but different. I'm saying try reading the Bible as the story of a certain people at a certain time as they grappled with identity and oppression and exile. Be disturbed by the awful things some of them did and awed by the incredible wisdom and compassion many of them showed. Be comforted by the ways in which the human condition has changed little and saddened by how the struggles of people to live together in a society persist. And then, frankly, put it down and read something else.

This is offputting for many, to say the least. But to allow the Bible to be the *entire* basis for your faith is to limit your relationship with God to what a single tradition established centuries ago. God is the God of everyone, right? What was God doing with people in the Western Hemisphere while the Israelites were being led out of Egypt? Was Jesus our one and only shot at meeting the human face of God so that if you lived in a part of the world that never got exposed to Jesus' story you were simply out of luck? Or could it be that the Bible records the traditions and experiences of a people who struggled mightily to survive repeated hardship?

From the other side, though, to ignore or dismiss the Bible is to miss out on an incredibly rich set of stories of God experiences. It contains brave social and political challenge, remarkably strong women, poetic witness of spirituality and the greatest example of peace, love and faithfulness until death found in any single human being in recorded history. If you read the Bible as stories from this tradition you can benefit from all that makes it still immensely relevant while not getting bogged down in all its very troubling aspects (I'm looking at you, Leviticus). There's a reason this tradition has endured.

So I encourage you to take another look at the Bible, and do so with a fresh set of eyes. To make the Bible less than it is may mean missing out on the power it can have in your life. However, to make it more than it is may mean alienation of others, stagnation of your own faith and misunderstanding of the messages the Bible contains. There are God experiences to be had all the time, within every faith and outside of any religion. Consider letting the Bible be part of your experience but not the final word.

The Language is the Kiss

July 23, 2013

There is something dramatic about blogging from a hospital bed, even though there is truly no drama to my situation on this day. I received a pacemaker this afternoon—something that was always going to be in my future due to my slow heart rate. But its recent deterioration in quality made it important to do now, and I feel great. Never below 50 bpm again!

The other reason it became important to do now is that I am going to have brain surgery on Thursday, and we needed to make sure my heart could take it. There is a mass on my left temporal lobe; it could be cancer, and it could be "radiation necrosis," or dead tissue from my radiation treatments two years ago. Either would be extremely rare, but I have been bestowed with one of them. I am emboldened by tonight's roommate, though. I won't go through the litany of crap he has going on, but one thing he shared is that he had a malignant tumor removed from his *brain stem* 14 years ago by the same neurosurgeon who is doing my "craniotomy." Sheesh. I like my chances for a simple clip and snip job.

Anyway. I have language "on my mind" these days, as the mass on my brain is in the area that controls language. There is very low risk of damage, but the very idea of not being able to communicate verbally is frightening. Language is precious to me, as you might expect. I took the title of this post from a favorite Indigo Girls song called, "The Language or the Kiss" about a relationship between one who overthinks everything and one who just feels. But I modified it because I believe that language expresses so much of our feelings and emotions, whether we intend it or not. As someone who fancies himself a writer, I am keenly aware of it, especially in certain contexts like this blog. But really in all contexts it's worth an awareness of how our use of language represents more than just the literal words we speak, and how it affects others and even ourselves.

Cancer, to be sure, has its own vocabulary. There is the clinical, of course, and any cancer patient gets used to his or her version of the radiology, oncology, CA-125 dance, including all the side effects and meds to manage them. But even in an environment where everybody is speaking the same language you have to be careful. My wife and I were at an oncology appointment a few months ago and were met by the friendliest of volunteers. He helped with coffee and offered directions, and so I looked at his name tag to thank him personally. It read, "Dennis Foster, volunteer, expires: 12/31/13." I suggested maybe a cancer center might not be the best place for a name tag with an expiration date; kind of sends the wrong message. Dennis gave a friendly smile but didn't seem to gather my implication.

There is another form of vocabulary around cancer, though, and it has to do with a more personal approach to dealing with the disease. From individuals and through organizations raising money for research we hear a great deal about the "fight" or "battle" against cancer. It usually stops short of all-out war, but the language is certainly hostile and violent. Who can blame them? The disease is unrelenting and frustrating and maddeningly creative in how it affects our bodies. It feels like an attack, so using language to characterize bringing the fight back at the disease makes perfect sense. I can only say that for me, personally, it has never worked. From initial diagnosis I have embraced language that is more peaceful. When it comes down to it, these cells are mine. They're part of this body with which I've been blessed. They may be misbehaving, but I accept them as part of who I am. Much more importantly, however, using this language of acceptance and peace keeps me in a peaceful place. That has been central to how I and my family have handled this ordeal. We stay centered and at peace and take each thing as it comes. This is by no means a criticism of anyone else's choice of language in facing cancer. It is simply our choice, and it's an intentional one. I do believe it's important to recognize how the language one uses may affect one's emotional and even spiritual state during a cancer journey.

I've been peeking at the next book my Sunday school class is going to be reading, and some of the ideas connected on the language front for me there, as well. In particular, I have been wrestling lately with the use of the word, "freedom." I am intentionally not political on this blog and will attempt to not stray here, but this one sticks with me. The book, *The Gospel According to America,* offers a surprisingly balanced view of American culture and its relationship to the Christian Gospel message. One early point in the book, though, is on America's tendency to view freedom on a very personal level. If we were, as a culture, to truly identify with the Christian message (and we do see that from some leaders and groups), wouldn't it be more of a social movement? Wouldn't freedom mean liberation for the collective on top of the personal freedoms we enjoy? When we were last in D.C., we were truly blown away by the FDR Memorial, and his famous "Four Freedoms" speech resonated especially: freedom of speech, freedom of worship, freedom from want, freedom from fear. Critical First Amendment personal rights augmented with a social conscience that elevates those who start at a disadvantage. Feels closer to the early Christian movement, but it's not how we often discuss "freedom" in America. The language matters.

Ultimately my reflections on language end up with the language we use for God. The first thing to recognize is that we are incapable of capturing the essence of God through human words, so I think it is incumbent upon us to acknowledge that any expressed view of God is incomplete. That may help keep us from getting too proprietary about our personal views. But at the same time, I think it's absolutely critical to be intentional about the language we do use. If terms like "Lord and Savior" are comfortable for you, it's good to be able to articulate to someone else why that works for you and how it affects your life. If you are more comfortable with "Holy Spirit," what does that mean to you and your daily life? If your concept of God is more Eastern and centered on a spirit or a collection of spiritual beings or forces, how do you talk about that and how it motivates your life? Many of us don't have a good vocabulary for our sense of the greater powers at work in the world, and "God" doesn't enter into it. Regardless, I think it's crucial to think through what sort of language best fits your concept of God or spiritual presence, as I think this can directly affect your spiritual journey and how it plays out for you day to day.

If you think I believe there is a single right answer here, clearly this is your first time reading the blog. Welcome. But let me prove it to you again.

I have a friend who is one of the most spiritual and peaceful people I have ever met. She shares this gift with me each time I see her just by being the presence she is. But she has done so much more for me by being so open in sharing her experience of God. She has spoken to me of having the very tangible feeling of sitting down to an intimate conversation with a very humanized version of a deity. I don't mean that in a diminishing way. It is downright exciting to hear her talk about an early morning coffee chat with God. It is personal and engaging and...lovely. And it's completely foreign to me. My spiritual journey has taken me in a very different direction, where my language for God is more about "the sacred" or "divine presence" and "source of life and love." It can still be personal in terms of my relationship, but it has more to do with communing with all that is (wow, I have become a hippie). Yet I gain so much from sharing experiences with my friend who views and experiences God in an entirely different way. I am gaining more of that through some of the responses to this blog. I treasure each one.

So think carefully about the language—your language—for how you experience that spiritual being or presence. Your language can become the kiss you give to someone else in their journey.

It's True Because It's Funny

August 15, 2013

Since my last post I had a very successful craniotomy to remove the mass on my left temporal lobe. Unfortunately, we learned that the mass is malignant tumor—carcinoma consistent with the (very unlikely) spread of my existing cancer to my brain. However, I am recovering very well. After Labor Day when my pacemaker allows it I will have a one-day radiation treatment and then go back on chemotherapy.

So it's fair to ask why there is a reference to something being "funny" in this post's title when I am dealing with stage four head and neck cancer with lymph node involvement and lung and brain metastasis complicated by an unhealthy heart rhythm that is now supported 100% of the time by an implanted device. (catching breath) The answer, like onions, ogres and parfaits, has layers. For starters, I tend to look for the humor in everything. Nothing irritates me more when I read a character-driven novel than when there is no humor. Life isn't like that. There is a funny side to almost every situation, whether the humor is broad, blue, dark...even tragic. Have you heard the saying, "comedy is tragedy plus time?" Well, I'm impatient.

There will be a tendency for some people to think that I use humor as a coping mechanism, a la M*A*S*H.

Those same people are likely to be unconvinced when I say this is not the case. But it truly is not. I simply like being (or trying to be) funny. I like it even more when others also think I'm being funny, but it isn't necessary. For example, after my first surgery left me paralyzed on the left side of my face I was driving with my younger daughter when "Poker Face" came on the radio. I sang along with Lady Gaga when she reached the chorus, changing the words to "my half poker face." Then I laughed out loud. The fact that my daughter also laughed and still brings it up to me is a wonderful bonus. I am fortunate to have a family that not only tolerates but participates in my irreverent treatment of my illness. On the day of my brain radiation I fully expect my wife to take pictures of me with the screws in my head holding the frame/halo that keeps me in place. She won't take them so that others can share in the experience and pray more specifically for my treatment. She will take them because I will look ridiculous.

I didn't realize it for awhile, but I think another reason I inject humor into my communications regarding my cancer journey is that I hope that it helps people realize 1) that I'm still me and dealing with this just fine and 2) that it's okay for them to be irreverent, too. In fact, I prefer it. Or, rather, I prefer people to be authentic. If humor is how they react to things, then humor is what I want. If it's tears, that's okay, too. I'm not fond of anger, but I'll take that, as well. I just want authenticity. So it would be dishonest of me to use humor if that's not what I feel. But I realize it's difficult for people to join in. It's a little like being a Jewish comedian who can make Jew jokes because he's Jewish, but it's not okay for us Gentiles. Well, that may not be the best example since I make Jew jokes to my Jewish friends, too. But you get the idea. I have come to terms with the fact that most people are not comfortable joining in with the cancer-related humor. I just hope people can understand that it is natural for me. And I hope they think it's funny.

I wish it didn't matter so much to me. My older daughter (an adult now) recently asked me if I ever considered writing comedy. I was stricken. I said, "I thought I did." Of course, she meant it as a compliment. "You're funny," she said. My heart leapt (pre-pacemaker). She might as well have told my old Jewish roommate that his mother was proud of him. (See? And he doesn't even read this.) Some of you know that I wrote a novel a few years ago, and some of you have even read it (though it remains unpublished) (*author's note: that novel and a second are to be self-published shorty after this blog anthology; see "About the Author" at the end of this book*). I have had people say it moved them, that they cried, that the small town in which it takes place really came to life. Generally, my response is, "And...?" You now know what I am waiting for them to say. Tell me the characters are thin; tell me the plot is unbelievable; tell me the prose is awkward; just, please, please tell me it's funny.

One thing that making or laughing at jokes about something can signify, I think, is a level of security with whatever that thing is. This may not be the case if humor is a form of deflection. But most often I think it shows a comfort level. This is certainly true for me with my illness. I'm not happy to have cancer, but I have embraced it. This is part of who I am now. And while I refuse to let it define me, I am happy to discuss it, write about it and make a seemingly endless stream of jokes about it and its effects on me. It is authentic. I realized somewhere along the line that I don't have the ability to play a role and be something I'm not for the sake of others when it comes to dealing with cancer. As Nick Hornby wrote in one of my favorite novels, "Sometimes we are judged by our one-offs." This is who I am with cancer.

I have long felt this way about religion and spirituality. If you can't poke fun at it, how secure are you in your faith? Notice I did not say, "make light of it." I think well-executed humor does exactly the opposite, shining a light on it in its full weightiness. When Sam Kinison said Jesus was up in heaven thumbing through the Bible saying, "Where did I say to build a water slide?" I laughed. And then I thought. When Christopher Moore in his novel *Lamb* had a teenage Jesus say, "I'm just f**king with you" or rave about how much he loves bacon, I was not offended. I laughed out loud and wished I had written the book myself. Don't even get me started on *The Book of Mormon.*

Embracing—and eventually creating—humor targeted at your particular belief system is not a sign of disloyalty. It's a sign of security. But it's also a sign of an open mind. Good comedy makes you think, and it's healthy to not let your faith become stagnant. Every experience of your life—even, or maybe especially, a life-threatening illness—reveals more to you about how your concept of God operates in the world. Don't let insecurity keep you from the richness of thought available to you from a good joke.

I Like My Chances

September 13, 2013

Pacemaker? Check. Brain surgery? Check. Gamma Knife radiosurgery? Check. Metastatic brain tumor? Well, check, but removed and cleaned up. I'm feeling good, although I'm out of shape and feeling it as I prepare for a cancer research fundraising bike ride (Pedal the Cause) on October 6th. 50 miles. Yeesh. Chemo starting again just before the ride, but I am committed to doing it.

So things have been piling up on us, and you might be wondering about the outlook. The fact is, however, that since I was originally diagnosed in February of 2011, one thing my wife and I have never requested is a prognosis. My ENT surgeon volunteered early on that with stage four parotid cancer we are usually talking about two-year survival rates instead of five-year...and the rate was 50/50 (making it especially poignant for me when the movie of that name came out). Whatever. They don't know the origin of my cancer, so they don't know which numbers to apply. And what if they did? What good would it do to have a number unless we were in an immediate "get your affairs in order" situation? Isn't it possible that those sometimes become self-fulfilling to some degree?

Regardless, we never asked, and we turned down

subsequent offers by doctors of survival time estimates. I know that the medical community (sadly) has a great deal of data on which to base its estimates. However, at the same time, cancer is mystifying. If it wasn't, then they would have a cure by now, or at least treatments that aren't so excruciating. And there would be more consistency in how people respond to those treatments. But instead much of it remains a mystery. I expect I will know when it's time to get those affairs in order. Until then I will treat myself as a going concern.

It's very different from the world of statistical probabilities. Very little mystery there. I recently completed a class on using models to improve our thinking, and we spent a lot of time looking at probabilities. I am going to assume those reading this will tend to be less dorky than I, so I won't bore you (much) with details. But here's an example: you might think that if someone in a casino wins 20 hands of blackjack in a row that Danny Ocean and his crew have invaded. Winning 20 in a row against the house is simply impossible. However, statistics tell us that if the casino has sufficient volume over a long enough period of time a streak of 20 in a row at some point is not only possible, it's practically inevitable. The problem comes when you are convinced that you're the person that's going to hit that streak. There goes the rent.

I think it is this kind of certainty that has always attracted me to math (see? dork). I love the fact that there's a single right answer. It's clean and definitive. I even liked statistics. If you keep your process inside of six standard deviations from the mean, your variation is going to be negligible. It's simple math (if not simple to accomplish), and it's certain.

Ironically, it is precisely this kind of certainty I find repellant in religious terms. This must be where the right side of my brain takes over. I don't begrudge anyone his or her deep faith or the clarity he or she might have about the order of things in the spiritual world. The "assurance of things hoped for and the conviction of things not seen" is not only comforting, it's very tangible to a great many people. I do not dispute that. But I think faith and knowledge are very different. I have a great many beliefs, but the things that I know for certain about God you can count on the fingers of Jim Abbott's right hand (I'll wait while you Google this proud Michigan reference).

You might say that my lack of certainty reflects a weak faith. Perhaps. But let me take this from a Christian perspective since that is the only one I have. If you are convinced of your Christian beliefs to the point where you feel compelled to denounce or at least dismiss other religions or variations of your Christian beliefs, how did you become so? Is it the utter consistency and straightforward teaching of the Bible? Forgive my sarcasm, but if the Bible provides you certainty of knowledge then you have—perhaps without realizing it—made a number of assumptions.

That's more like economics than math or statistics. Ever hear the joke about how economists get out of a deep hole? First they assume a ladder. A good example of an assumption one might make about the Bible is that many particulars about Jesus actually matched Hebrew prophecy rather than having been crafted that way by the author decades later to communicate a message to the Jewish people. (spoiler alert) *I don't know*, but I tend to think it was the latter...and I don't even think that's a bad thing.

This is one reason that religion sometimes scares me. Too often I think religion is about absolutes: here is what we all agree we believe, and that's the end of it. I feel extremely fortunate to have a faith community that welcomes questions and has room for diversity of belief, but I know many Christian communities are not so flexible. This is one reason it has become so fashionable to say, "I'm not religious. I'm spiritual." The world of spirituality is a world of mystery, and mystery defies certainty. That is not only attractive to people, it's healthy.

Of course, this is just from a Christian point of view. Here's a number: 75% of all (not just "religious") Americans identify as "Christian." In that environment it is easy to lose perspective. What of the billions of people in the world who follow other religions? Are the numbers still in favor of Christian certainty? I am not saying that one should not believe something just because others believe something else. But isn't it possible those other religions—not to mention thinkers who do not identify with a religion—have something valuable to teach us?

In a way I think my developing ability to embrace mystery in my spiritual life has prepared me to embrace the mystery of my disease. Certainly cancer is a mystery I hope and believe will be solved someday. Not so the spiritual questions. So without answers what is left to us? Study. Questioning. Discussion. Prayer. And most of all: action. You may not know for certain the answers to all your questions, but you feel a spirit moving you. Follow it. If I try to follow the example of Jesus rather than worrying about whether he was born in Bethlehem, then I will love my enemies, care for the outcast and place people over possessions. I can't know the exact probability that this is what God wants from me...but I like my chances.

Christian, Heal Thyself

October 14, 2013

As I move out of the healing process from brain surgery and back into chemotherapy, which raises its own challenges, I am drawn to thoughts of Jesus and his healing miracles. At least to this point in my cancer journey I have not found myself wondering why no healing miracle has presented itself to me. It isn't something I expect, even while I also do not believe such things are impossible. I'm not being noble when I say I wonder more why daily victims of hunger or tyranny or extreme abuse around the world are not first visited by healing long before it would reach me.

Let's be clear on what I mean by "healing miracles." I am referring to the intervention in the physical world by a deity directly or through an instrument—the most prominent example in Christianity being the healing acts of Jesus described in the Bible. These are the explicit, unquestionable demonstrations of God's healing power, as opposed to those unlikely or surprising turnarounds that ailing patients make that the doctors cannot fully attribute to their treatments. I think there are many things that appear to violate natural law because we do not yet understand nature well enough to explain them. Science hasn't caught up. I am not ruling out the supernatural here; I am simply saying it is not to these relatively minor detours from the expected biological path that I am referring. I'm talking about the "stand up and walk" and "your faith has made you well" variety.

The nagging question for me on these tier one healings is why they don't happen anymore. Jesus wasn't the only one who reportedly performed them. Why didn't God allow those to whom Jesus gave this power to share that power, in turn, with subsequent generations? If the purpose was to demonstrate that they held God's power and to draw people to the early Christian movement, why not keep it going? Surely we did not and have not run out of the need to draw people toward God.

It will challenge the thinking of many Christians to consider that one explanation for God's apparent moratorium on such miracles is that they never happened in the first place.

This is not to suggest that Jesus did not perform any healing. Quite the contrary. But I am suggesting that Jesus needed no supernatural powers to heal. Instead he needed extraordinary courage and compassion. John Dominic Crossan, a noted biblical scholar and thinker, references anthropologists in distinguishing between *disease* and *illness*. To put it simply, disease is biological malfunctioning while illness is society's reaction to the disease. Crossan suggests that what Jesus did was heal, for example, the leper's illness rather than his disease. He did this by validating the leper's humanity and calling for the abolition of his social alienation. Jesus' message was all about removing the labels and distinctions that separate people and putting everyone on equal ground—sitting at the table together (you know, cuz they sat on the ground).

If you are one who is challenged by this idea, let me encourage you to set aside for a moment the question of whether Jesus healed disease. We will not all agree on that point, but I'm betting we can all agree that Jesus did heal illness as Crossan defines it. I worry that if we focus too much on whether Jesus cured disease we miss the healing that was truly at the center of his message; the healing that we, too, can perform.

Times are different, of course. For the most part, at least in developed nations, we no longer view the diseased as unclean or outcasts. I am aware there are exceptions, the most glaring of which will lead me in a moment to one of my central points. But in my case, for example, I have not been ostracized due to my disease. Quite the opposite, in fact. It feels as though I have become a better, more likable person in some people's eyes since my diagnosis—or at least people have become more expressive with their affection and/or less so with their derision. Either way, I am not complaining.

So what is our modern day equivalent to disease that

creates this illness of public scorn? Who is unclean in the eyes of society and in need of healing? I wish there was only one answer to that question (if there is to be one at all), but I know there are potentially many depending on the culture and environment in which you live. It could be race, religious belief, disability, size...but I am going to focus briefly on one that is among the most rampant. The glaring exception I mentioned above is HIV/AIDS, and the reason I think it can still generate as much illness of alienation as it does is not because of the disease itself but because of the lifestyle with which people still associate it.

Some good friends of mine told me about their seven-year-old, Catholic-schooled son volunteering out of the blue that he thought homosexuals needed a leader like Martin Luther King to help with the gay marriage fight. I find it very instructive—as well as hopeful—that our young people a) recognize this as a civil rights issue and b) are bewildered as to why it is an issue at all. I share their bewilderment. Even if one uses a faithful reading of the bible to determine that homosexuality is a sin, why this sin? Of all the things the (ancient, pre-enlightenment, fallibly human in my view) bible tells us are sins, why are people so rabid about this private, victimless one that has only to do with loving another person? I have my ideas on the answer, and you likely do, too, but I will leave that discussion for another time. I will just share that I do not believe it is a sin at all, much less one that requires our intervention.

As I have said before, I view Christianity as striving to follow the example of Jesus. And while in my current state I would love a good old-fashioned disease healing, I prefer to focus on the example I can actually follow. I can be a healer. Every time I openly demonstrate that I do not recognize or accept the lines that divide, stratify and alienate us, I am healing a pervasive illness. When I embrace another human being and affirm his or her lifestyle as every bit as valid as my own, I am doing my best to be a Christian. Perhaps the only remaining question is who is really being healed.

The Sound of One Voice

November 15, 2013

I had a bad night last week.

It should have been a good night. It was a pretty fall night in Manhattan, and I had time to myself to do a little exploring, which I did. Never mind that I was in town to see an oncologist the next day. I wasn't expecting any earth-shattering news; just keeping another doctor in the loop because I was coming to NY for work anyway. So I should have enjoyed walking through Chelsea and the West Village on a cool fall night, watching people in Washington Square Park and gathering food from various vendors at a food market in Herald Square. And, in fact, I did enjoy those things. But throughout the night I felt an undercurrent of melancholy (yeah, that's right; pretentious-sounding, but precise).

This may not seem all that remarkable given my circumstances, but it's actually quite rare for me. So I ruminated for a time on the potential cause and decided it had a couple of layers. On the surface I was feeling my mortality. Walking around the city doing things I don't normally get to do represented to me a different Jason—or at least a different direction my life could take. I don't mean that I wish I could move to NYC; I mean that, more generally, I wish that I could reinvent myself and take a very different path if I decided I wanted to. I felt frustrated that my illness will very likely deprive me of those decades of living an alternative Jason Hill experience.

Beneath that layer was carryover from our Sunday school class the day before. We were talking about music, and the author of the book we're reading spent a lot of time on R.E.M. As leader of this particular study I was reading some passages from the book, and I surprised myself by my reaction to discussion of the song "Try Not To Breathe." The lyrics speak of an old man to whom no one will listen but who wants to be heard. His eyes "have seen things that you will never see," and he wants to witness. He wants you to remember. I don't know if anyone in class noticed, but I got choked up reading this. I realized the next night as I felt the weight of my circumstance that I am an old man. And I want you to remember.

But what is so special about my perspective? Have I seen things that you will never see? Of course I have, if only because I saw them through my eyes. My perspective is special to the extent that each one of us has a unique way of seeing one another, events, the world. I spend more than my share of time talking about how we should think more socially, be it as Christians or otherwise, Americans or otherwise...just as human beings. But this should not obscure the value of the individual.

Most would argue that in America recognition of the value of the individual is not a problem; in fact, it's foundational. Our Constitution emphasizes individual liberties. Our system of capitalism emphasizes acting in one's own best interests rather than that of the collective. Electoral college notwithstanding, each of us gets a vote. Each of us has the right to speak out, to disagree, to protest. No, for better or for worse—and there is plenty of each—philosophically, the individual is king in the United States.

I think the problem is noise. The Internet has given everyone a platform, but when @bigballs23 comments that your YouTube video "is like a beer fart traped in a compac car," (sp) are you enriched? Mr. (I'm assuming) bigballs may have a great deal of insight to share with the world, but this isn't where he's sharing it. With apologies to my daughter, whom I love and who has a great deal of value to contribute to the lives of others, I gain little from her tweet about her annoyance with people who don't know how to use the self-service checkout lane at the supermarket (#gotoacashier). It takes greater and greater effort to weed out the inane bullshit—including that which we, ourselves, generate—to find the gems individuals have to offer. "Selective listening" usually has a negative connotation, but it might be what saves us.

Speaking specifically of the spiritual realm, as I try to do here, I encourage you to make the effort. Find the right venues where people speak reasonably and intelligently, whether in person or online. Challenge yourself to engage in conversation with people who see religion or spirituality differently than you do. Benefit from the things they have seen that you will never see. Listen. And speak. Or sing. Or write. Share what you see and enrich someone else. The pastor of my church talks about the importance of "one" every Sunday, and I finally get it. As a faith community we are powerful not because we are a COLLECTION of individuals but because we are a collection of INDIVIDUALS. I am grateful to my church for letting me be an individual, asking questions and challenging beliefs while still being valued.

And I am grateful to you for reading this. You have decided that the messages here cut through the noise to a sufficient degree that perhaps your life is enriched as a result. I hope so. I do want to share my words, and I do want you to remember. But I also want to listen.

Whether it's from the Wailin' Jennys or Barry Manilow, we know that the sound of one voice is most powerful when it joins other individual voices in song. Please sing with me. (#onevoice #noisecancelling #antibigballs)

My Bondage Fetish

December 9, 2013

On the news this past week of the death of Nelson Mandela it is almost too easy for every writer, commentator and half-assed blogger to co-opt Mandela's life and message for his or her own selfish purposes. Almost. Far be it from me to overlook the easy path. I'll take the road more traveled by and let you decide if it makes a difference.

The story of Mandela's imprisonment for 27 years, 18 of them in a tiny cell on Robben Island, brings into sharp focus for most of us the many freedoms we enjoy. This is an obvious takeaway from all of the stories this week: to appreciate what we have and to take a good look at ourselves to see how far we would be willing to go to advocate for the freedoms of our fellow human beings. Good takeaways but not at all where my mind has gone. No, I find myself obsessing not on our freedoms but on our own respective enslavements.

I forced myself to write this entry now because I received some bad news this week. The chemotherapy drug I have been taking has not retarded the growth of the tumors in my lungs, and, in fact, a tumor has sprouted near one of my vertebrae. This is the first bone involvement; no symptoms yet but obviously not an encouraging sign. In order to be authentic—as I have asked people to be with me—I thought it important to communicate now, from this mental and emotional place, rather than waiting for my optimism to fully regenerate. Not every week is a good one.

A cancer diagnosis can cause a feeling of acute helplessness. So much is both unexplained and out of my control that I find myself actively searching for things that I *can* do. I try to exercise as I am able and eat right not just because they are generally good ideas but also in order to regain strength to prepare for the "next thing," whether a surgery or treatment or symptom. I find time to read and write in order to continually explore my spirituality and exercise my mind as threats against it are no longer idle. And I try to make time to do the things I enjoy, though this week's onslaught of winter reminds me that I have to be more creative this time of year. I mean, seriously, why do we live like this? How can there be such population concentrations this far north of the equator? Are Canadians biologically different from us or just mentally disabled? I think my nipples are going to be erect and chafed until April....

But I digress.

My point is that, if I let it, cancer will become my master and I its slave. I mean, it wouldn't be to national debt proportions of slavery, but still. I am a slave to cancer if I let it define who I am, take away my ability to choose how I live my life and deprive me of my rights to laughter, excitement and anticipation. Slaves, apartheid victims and prisoners like Mandela could not choose to deny power to their oppressors except as it related to their spirit. My life is far too fortunate and privileged for me to equate my experience to theirs, but in this small way they are similar. I cannot remove cancer from my life, but I can keep it from making me its spiritual slave.

Lest you think I am getting carried away with myself, I submit that I am not alone in this. In fact, I submit that we all have our chains that bind us. Some elude identification, while others are as plain as the rash on my face.

The contributors to the "Living the Questions" class, which I have referenced before, suggest that the Bible has three primary themes: sin/forgiveness, exile/reconciliation and bondage/deliverance. In the Christian faith I think we tend to focus on the first of these a bit too much, always talking about our sinful nature and the need for us to repent to be saved. But since I first heard these themes stated I have been preoccupied with the idea of our bondage. Have just a cursory knowledge of the Bible or even Cecil B. Demille and you can easily identify the source of the theme. Slavery was a fact of life throughout the Bible, and the deliverance from slavery in Egypt is the central event of the Jewish tradition.

At first blush this may seem to put distance between us and the Bible, making it more historical and less relatable. But I think it does exactly the opposite if we look more closely. We are fortunate through birth and/or the sacrifices of others to be free of slavery as the Israelites knew it. But we allow ourselves to become slaves to other aspects of our lives. For me it has long been financial security. I have been fortunate to never have worked a job that I hated (at least not since the paint line at the IPG factory in Reading, MI, summer 1990. One whistleblower and OSHA would have brought that place to its knees. The plant manager's last name was Bonecutter, for God's sake). At the same time, however, I have never had the courage to pursue a true passion, whether writing or anything else. I have allowed myself to be bound by the need to be a responsible breadwinner. I have made career decisions that have cost me greater financial opportunities, but I have also avoided decisions that would have caused me to take financial steps backward but could have helped me contribute to the ongoing creation, if you will.

At this point I run the risk of sounding like a whiner. The truth is that I look at my life and smile genuinely (if crookedly). But I relate to the biblical theme of bondage/deliverance because I recognize it in my own life. It is that which keeps me from spiritual fulfillment and wholeness, and deliverance is elusive.

What are your chains? It's different for each of us.

Addiction? Pursuit of money? Damaged relationships? What is your source of pain, of brokenness...of separation from God in whatever form that takes for you? What keeps you from your spiritual center? Whatever it is, I do not have an easy answer for deliverance. People tell me the answers are all in the Bible, and that may be true for some. It is not for me. But I think spiritual exploration and meditation can help us identify our chains and begin the path to deliverance.

My premise with cancerandchrist is that spiritual certainty is dangerous and limiting. Here I add that it can be enslaving. An unwillingness to acknowledge that there is no single right answer to spiritual questions can become the shackles that restrain your growth. That bondage becomes tangible when you are faced with evidence that runs counter to your entrenched beliefs. Instead of allowing those religious or spiritual beliefs to chain you down, why not use spiritual exploration to help deliver you from whatever other personal bondage you face?

My unwillingness to let cancer own me has crystallized for me the other bondage I have allowed in my life. I thank you for reading this, as pursuing my passions for writing and spiritual contemplation moves me step by step closer to freedom.

Do You Hear What I Kinda Hear?

January 8, 2014

One of the centerpieces of my ability to remain peaceful through this cancer journey is my decision to take things as they come. I don't know what to expect, and I don't want to know. Unfortunately, I strayed from that approach in December. Blame it on science...and arrogance.

When I went in for my scans in early December I was sure that there was a new problem with my brain but that the chemotherapy drug was working. I was having mild headaches reminiscent of the ones that led to discovery of my brain tumor in June. Meanwhile, all signs pointed to effective chemotherapy. I had the worst rash my doctor had seen of anyone on the drug yet taking medication for the rash. Everyone said that was a good sign. My doctor at Sloan Kettering agreed the drug made sense as a next step. And we even did DNA testing to pinpoint how my tumors behave, and that testing pointed to the drug I was taking. IBM predicts this will become more and more common and even touts an ability to do it to some extent today.

I'm an IBMer. Let's build a Smarter Planet. But let's not get ahead of ourselves.

As it turns out, my brain scan was completely clear

while the chemotherapy was completely ineffective. I really can't blame anyone else for the disappointment/pleasant surprise. I had done such a good job of guiding my doctors by being attuned to my body and symptoms that I began to believe I knew what was happening. I have now been jarred back into reality, which is that I don't know anything. Uncertainty welcomed me home, and there was peace on my little patch of earth for the Christmas season.

It can go the other way, though, can't it? The deeper the roots of our certainty the more disorienting it can be when we are faced with contradictory evidence. This can lead us away from peace and into a state either of denial or distress. I was certain the Michigan Wolverine football team was poised for great things in 2013. Reality was jolting, and though I was never in denial all season I did have my share of distress.

Perhaps nowhere is this more true than in our spiritual lives, given how central these beliefs are to our very beings. Now, the last thing I want to do is negate or disparage anyone's beliefs. Yet doesn't it sometimes seem that religion is the last bastion of primitive thought? Let's be careful here, though. It may be easy for the intellectual to turn up his or her nose at the creationist, but certainty comes in many forms. Of what spiritual beliefs are you certain? That there is no god? That God has a plan that accounts for everything that happens? That those who don't accept Jesus go to hell? Are you sure? I suppose it helps that there is no evidence one way or the other for these sorts of beliefs...or is there? When someone you respect and admire holds a conflicting belief that might jar you a little. When something happens that feels inconsistent with your world view that might jar you a lot.

I've written before about the dangers of certainty and the peace that comes with accepting mystery. But Christmastime magnifies it for me. Setting aside the secular traditions, we have built a culture around the religious mythology of Christmas, from the angels to the virgin to the manger to the star. I use "mythology" here not to mean invented, necessarily, but traditional and iconic. Yet for so many the very meaning of Christmas is tied to the details of this story that requires two somewhat conflicting Gospel accounts to construct. I love the Christmas story, but I hear it as legend--it doesn't matter to me how much of it is historically accurate.

Let me share an alternative version of the Christmas story, and you take your own certainty temperature as you read it.

Mary was a young, faithful Jewish girl who prayed daily and was known throughout Nazareth to be both gentle and disciplined. She fell in love with an older man named Joseph, and almost immediately following their nuptials Mary discovered she was with child. Each night as her baby grew inside her Mary would dream of the future—of the family she would nurture and the blessings she would enjoy. Each day she would offer prayers of thanksgiving and sing songs of hope and joy.

When the time came to deliver the baby, Joseph and Mary found themselves alone. They had no surviving family in Nazareth, and the other women in the town felt alienated by Mary's radiance even as they admired it. Joseph pleaded with their neighbors, and an elderly woman at last agreed to come and assist. Mary's labor was difficult, but the baby boy was born healthy and given the name Jesus. The elderly neighbor wrapped Jesus in a blanket and handed him to Mary. Both Mary and Joseph, as they gazed at the tiny boy, knew Jesus was destined to do great things. He had a light in his eyes that gave him an aura of spirituality and spoke of an understanding of the love they felt for him.

For many years it was only his parents who could see how remarkable Jesus was. They raised him to obey Jewish Law but also to think for himself and to show compassion and love to others. But it was not long before Joseph and Mary felt that Jesus was teaching them. That light that they saw in his infant eyes blossomed into a profound presence that some found disturbing but most found undeniably magnetic. He radiated a sense of peace and even as an adolescent seemed more connected to the spirit of God than anyone his parents knew. This boy would grow to become a gifted and controversial teacher, a revolutionary and most of all one of the greatest examples of love the world has ever known. He would eventually die for his faithfulness to that principle of love above all else.

No census, no Bethlehem, no manger. No angels, no shepherds, no star. No wise men. No virgin. I love Christmas and the imagery that goes with the story, but when I hear it, this is what is in my mind. I do not offer it as the gospel truth—I don't know what actually happened. I offer it as an alternative to certainty: what if this *is* the truth? Would you be less of a Christian? More? If Jesus was a very, very special human—but only a human—does that necessarily change your faith? Isn't the message of love and peace and compassion the same? Might it not even be liberated from the restrictions of right belief?

In all honesty, I also offer this because this is where I am on my spiritual journey. Some will believe that I am condemned to hell. Some may feel sorry for me for my lack of faith. Some will find themselves in a similar place. But perhaps some will consider these ideas and at least begin to loosen their grip on their religious convictions.

Nobody knows the answers. Is there room for me at the inn of your certainty?

God Makes Me Sick

January 20, 2014

This past week was a strange one. I had a sharp pain and hard spot where my kidneys are, and my doctor thought I should have an x-ray. It turned out to be nothing, but it served as a reminder to me.

You see, at this juncture I am fully recovered from my brain tumor and am tolerating the chemotherapy quite well. I have no pain from the tumors in my spine and no shortness of breath from the tumors in my lungs. In short, I have no symptoms of the disease that has infiltrated so many places in my body—only acute and lingering side effects of surgeries and treatments. But I know this will not last forever.

Ever since I found the second nodule right above my clavicle just one week out from my initial surgery I have understood that this disease would most likely take my life prematurely. As the surgeon put it, I have a "bad process" going on in my body. Now, it's almost three years since my initial diagnosis, and I still don't have any symptoms. I'm doing very well. But with brain and lung metastasis and now bone involvement, the writing is on the visceral pleura.

Hopefully you've learned by reading past entries that this does not mean I have "given up" or resigned myself to imminent death. Far from it. I continue to do everything I can to extend my life, including the consideration of some unsavory options down the road if necessary (I'm talking about tough side effects, not black market organs or something—relax). And with advances being made all the time, who knows? Still, I am realistic.

This week's experience reminded me that at some point I will turn a corner...in the wrong direction. Once I become symptomatic the calculus of treatment changes somewhat, and it's possible that things could deteriorate rapidly. I have been through a lot in the last three years, but I have continued to work full time, exercise, travel, etc., pretty much uninterrupted except by surgery recoveries. I do not look forward to the day that changes.

The other reminder this week's experience provided was that of a question I've received: some version of, "How can you believe in a God that allows this kind of disease?" Most of this blog has come from an assumption of a belief in God and has argued for an open-minded rethinking of traditional religious views. I've even directly addressed the nature of God and why God allows bad things to happen, but what about the most basic, traditional view of them all? Why do I believe in God in the first place?

Let me start by affirming that I do, in fact, believe in God. It is as fundamental to my life as breathing (which seems like a better analogy than a beating heart, since I get mechanical assistance with that). When I go too long without doing or experiencing something that moves me to feel God's presence, my mood suffers. I think it's even possible my physical health suffers. As I have said before, I see God as the source of love and life in the world, and when I experience something that takes me to a "thin place" (credit: Marcus Borg)—whether through a loving act by another person, the mysterious beauty of nature or "When Doves Cry" coming on the radio—I experience God.

God carries a lot of baggage we have heaped on God from the Bible and subsequent councils and decrees by the institutional church. As one of the contributors to "Living the Questions" put it, "Tell me about this God you don't believe in. Chances are I don't believe in that God, either." Certainly the very concept of God, no matter how you define it, is beyond human comprehension. All of our characterizations fall well short—more John Grisham than John Steinbeck. But even if we take this as a given, how do we work ourselves back to why we believe in God at all?

There are the emotional arguments, where we believe we feel God's presence or somehow "just know." There are the transformational arguments where perhaps we have had specific experiences where God "washed over us" and redirected our lives—the born again experience. There are the interventional arguments where we believe God caused something to happen that only God could have caused (like me not getting into Northwestern Business School—that had to be God, right?) There are the fundamentalist arguments—or, rather, *the* fundamentalist argument: the Bible says so.

No doubt there are many, many more, but let me add just one additional: the logical argument, working backwards from the present to the creation of the universe. Evolution is real, but who created the natural laws that make evolution work? If the universe was created by a big bang, from where did the matter come to generate that bang? Something must have generated the first something out of nothing.

This is where my head produces a big bang of its own. And that's okay, because I am actually more moved to belief in God by the wonders of the ongoing creation than I am by "in the beginning." I am fascinated by science and nature, and nowhere do I find this more compelling than the intricacies of the human body. I have been exposed to a great deal more detail as a result of my illness, and each time I learn something new I am reminded of the Indigo Girls lyric, "No way construction of this tricky plan was built by other than a greater hand." In a number of ways, most having to do with my experiences of the love of others and a more vivid understanding of myself, my cancer journey has brought me closer to God. But in this way—through my fascination with the disease's behavior in my body—cancer has actually deepened my *belief* in God.

But if God is light and love, how can cancer be of God? I do not know that there is a good answer to this, but I was intrigued by one attempt. I don't have the reference handy, but one of our Sunday school classes at church studied a lesson that described the "shadow side" of free will and used cancer as a specific example. The idea is that not only humans but every living thing—including individual cells—have freedom, if not conscious will. They will pursue their self-interests, and sometimes this causes mutations resulting in what we view as disease.

A little out there, maybe, but fascinating. And it resonates with me because it aligns somewhat with my own view of my cancer. I don't see myself as the victim of some evil force that is fighting with God's love and protection. I see myself as experiencing another aspect of God's creation that is mysterious and complex and far beyond my understanding. It is painful and frightening and brutal—as much for its impact on those I love as for its effects on me—and I wish it would leave me. But that doesn't necessarily mean it is not of God.

I don't believe in God *because* I have cancer. But I don't believe in God any less as a result of having the disease. I don't expect everyone to agree with or even understand this perspective, but what I do hope is that you take some time to think about why you believe in God—or why you don't. And I encourage you to go beyond a simple statement of faith. I'm not knocking it; have faith—or don't. But understand why.

It's All About Me...Isn't It?

February 9, 2014

When the bad news begins to pile up on a cancer patient, said patient might be forgiven for becoming a little "me-focused." In my case, last month I learned that the second consecutive chemotherapy I tried was not helping. Not only did the tumors continue to grow, but I also developed fluid in my lung as the disease advanced further. So as of last Thursday I am back on the hard stuff—same chemo I took in 2012.

So, yes, nothing positive there. One deals with something like this and might be expected to turn inward, to withdraw, or at least to "play the cancer card" a little more often. I can speak only for myself, but this urge can be powerful, especially in the first days after treatment; queasiness can be a consuming distraction. At the same time, however, succumbing to that urge is the very last thing I truly want to do.

The first time I went through this course of treatment the dose was higher. Around days four and five I was literally telling people that I had discovered the real purpose of chemotherapy: to make you not care if you die. An uncharacteristically melodramatic overstatement, to be sure, but that gives you an idea of how I was feeling. It was during this very time that a friend from church called me to ask if I could give her a ride to the hospital and back to see her doctor and pick up a prescription. "I figured you'd like to do something for someone else," she told me. I would like to think that this is a vibe I give off, but I suspect this has more to do with her general outlook than with her view of me as a person. In fact, it was exactly what I needed. I was uncomfortable and nauseated, but at the same time I was energized by the opportunity.

I do my best to keep that experience in mind. When I hit my nadir—when my cell counts bottom during a course of treatment—I don't feel like doing anything. It is then that I am especially sure to get up and move to get the red blood cells I have circulating. More generally, when the chemo clouds set in I try not to curl into the fetal position. I do not always succeed here, and I don't begrudge anyone else their withdrawal into themselves. But I *try* to turn things around—whether by helping with our church youth group, giving an elderly friend a ride or inviting my nephew over for a Star Wars movie marathon. Of course, these actions are not completely selfless—especially the last one—but that's the point. I get something out of it, too, and turning the focus out away from myself actually diminishes the effects of my symptoms.

One of the things I got the chance to do in January was accompany our church youth group, including my daughter, to a large youth rally in Springfield, MO.

Over 2,500 youth and adults gathered for what they call "WOW" or "Weekend of Worship." It's a series of professional acts—including bands, a comedy duo and a magician—leading the group in worship activities. Each group or individual shared a witness story and a message as part of the act. Without exception the message was about Jesus' role in the life of the individual. Jesus entered the person's life and set him or her on the right path, and the message to the youth was to do the same. It was all about the personal relationship with Christ and moral living. Virtually nowhere was there a message about how we are to treat others and care for those in need. (To be fair, there was a pitch for fundraising for Imagine No Malaria at the very end, but the silent auction had been so silent that I was not aware of it until they announced the winners.)

Now, clearly I am not the target audience at an event like this. If I needed any reminding of that it came in the form of a t-shirt being sold there that said, "My ancestors weren't monkeys, they were rednecks!" I get that our youth are attempting to find themselves and their spiritual beliefs, and this group is looking to guide them to Jesus. I cannot argue with the role model. However, what better time than during the formation of one's spiritual identity to be introduced not only to the ethereal idea of Jesus in one's life but to his actual life and teachings?

I don't want to pick on the rally. It was a powerful

event with a solid message. Too often, however, I think the more conservative or traditional view of Christianity can come across as too much Ten Commandments and not enough Greatest Commandment. Ultimately, if we are to follow the example of Christ, it must go well beyond our personal relationship with him. The Gospel message is one of unconditional love—not tolerance; not even acceptance. *Love*. We have piled a lot of supposedly necessary specific beliefs on top of that to define what a Christian is, but the core of it is really quite simple.

I come at this from a Christian perspective, but no matter your spiritual or religious perspective aren't we all better served by an individual spirituality that is a little less...individual? I am most inspired by religions when I see them at work in the world—and I see that a lot. From our own church's youth mission trips to the massive efficiency of Catholic Charities to all the examples between and beyond the Christian faith there is no shortage of organized religious participation in helping those in need. Some religions, like Islam, are very community-based and less individual. But I would guess that most of us are guilty of—at least at times—thinking of our spiritual lives exclusively as they relate to us alone.

This may seem pretty basic, and many of you are way ahead of me on this. But if we take it a step farther it becomes more difficult for most. Where I find the example of Christ most compelling and intimidating is in his consistent response to persecution with love. No matter what pain or humiliation people inflicted on Jesus, his response was to love them. I don't care whether you believe in Jesus or the bible or even God—that's a high bar. I know I struggle with it. But what greater calling than to show love to someone who is mistreating you? One way to look at it is that creation is good. People, as part of that creation, are inherently good and must have been damaged, themselves, to be mistreating you as they are. They don't just need love; they *deserve* it, as we all do. Another way to look at it is that responding with love to those who hurt you can only be a positive for YOU. It allows you to begin to let go of the anger that will otherwise fester inside you.

Easy to say. Difficult to accomplish. The truth is that I am not doing nearly enough in my life for other people, cancer or no cancer. And I am usually at my best when I show tolerance to those that I see harming me or others; demonstrating love is too often beyond my reach. But I hope to initiate some change and maybe even chronicle it here. Perhaps you will join me. Whether you're dealing with the effects of cancer treatments or financial hardship or relationship strains or anything else, I encourage you to try with me to lean into it. Don't withdraw. Find a way to share some love with someone else. And if you're up for it, maybe even send some love the way of the person causing you pain, if that's what is happening. My experience is that when I'm able to take the focus off myself then I end up focusing less on the pain and living more fully. Cancer may take my life, but not yet.

So I guess it is all about me after all. I knew it.

My Only Friend, The End

March 6, 2014

On any journey one at some point begins to think about the end. On a cancer journey you can avoid this for long stretches—of hours, not days. But understand that there are many endings to consider short of "the big one."

Thursday I go back for treatment again after four weeks. It was supposed to be three weeks between doses, but I had a business trip last week and pushed treatment out. So I am feeling pretty good: energy is good, taste is decent, and I haven't had any digestive issues for three weeks. Tonight, though, I am feeling the end of all that. I will be fine during treatment; then I'll go home and get queasy, and over the coming days my fingertips will get a little more numb and probably start to hurt, my tongue will get filmy and gross, my fingernails will start to decay, my legs will feel heavy, and my stamina will diminish. I will mostly feel okay; I'll work and exercise (slowly) and do all the day-to-day things. But I will be off. Feeling good will end. And it will accumulate across doses as long as this medication is helping.

Which leads me to another ending. Before my next dose at the end of the month I will get a scan that will tell us whether I am responding to this chemo drug.

We have held off on returning to these drugs because they are more toxic, but other alternatives have been ineffective. Once this drug no longer works on me or I can no longer handle it (I'm betting the former occurs before the latter), we will have very limited options left. This course of treatment will end, and we will turn from the unpleasant but known to the unknown.

At some point being asymptomatic of the disease will end (the fluid in my lung having given me a preview). At some point my ability to work will end, and I will need to figure out how to spend my days. At some point I will no longer be able to take vacations with my family. At some point even day-to-day things will become difficult. And, at some point, I will encounter "the big one."

We need some new euphemisms for this, don't you think? I will offer a few here, but please come up with your own.

- Taking a selfie with Jesus
- Pouring water on the campfire
- Clicking the ruby slippers
- Wrapping up the burrito (no, that sounds like something else)

You don't have to be on a cancer journey to be preoccupied, at times, with endings. Sometimes all you have to do is go to church.

We're starting Lent today, and while Good Friday

remembers the end of Jesus' life, Easter is primarily focused on resurrection and a fresh start for everyone. Sorry, I mean a fresh start for all Christians. And the Cadbury corporation. Yet even at this time of year many of the messages are not about a beginning but an end, as in the final disposition of our respective souls. Jesus died so that we may be forgiven, the teaching goes; the ultimate sacrifice that washed away our sins and assured our salvation. Through grace, then, we are saved. We don't have to do anything—cannot, in fact, earn it. We only have to believe the exact right thing.

Am I oversimplifying? In some cases, certainly. I recognize every denomination and every church has a slightly different interpretation and message emphasis. However, I have been a United Methodist my entire life, and this is roughly what I have retained from countless lessons and sermons, at least at a high level. Quibble with the details, but this is broadly the Christian message.

For all our emphasis as Christians on our individual final dispositions, we often shy away from taking a hard look at the BIG ending. The end for everyone on earth. The end of days. The end of the world as we know it. The church doesn't ignore it, to be sure. Many church congregations recite every week, "from thence he shall come to judge the quick and the dead." Well, you better be awfully quick. We don't spend much time reading Revelation because it's hard, but the theology is clear. Jesus, who loves everyone and responded to all persecution and violence with love is coming back with a sword to Sort. This. Shit. Out.

I am not going to pretend to be an expert on Revelation. I've studied it some, and I plan to study it more (I know what you're thinking: you better hurry up). But does the violent Second Coming image of Jesus jibe with your image of him from the Gospels? Me neither. Recently, though, I have been reading Matthew, and I was surprised by how many references Jesus is said to have made to the violent end that will come to those who are not righteous. I mean, I've never gnashed my teeth, but it doesn't sound pleasant. This is a very Jewish point of view and so also very Matthew, writing for his Jewish audience. But clearly you don't even have to dive into the murky depths of Revelation to uncover the doctrine of ultimate judgment and punishment. So maybe this teaching is spot on.

Or...

...maybe this was Matthew putting words in the mouth of Jesus.

...maybe Revelation was about the end of the Roman Empire, not the world, and the anticipation of the kickass Messiah the Jews always thought they would get.

...maybe this is what Jesus thought would happen but, being human, he was wrong.

I will leave that last matzo ball hanging out there without elaboration and hope my Christian readers' heads don't explode. And the alternate view of Revelation has a great deal of scholarly and clergy support. Don't get me started on the idea of The Rapture, which is not even biblical. But my primary point, as it is so often, is that *we don't know*. Each of us has some idea—or no idea—about what awaits us at the end of time. But what I think we have to avoid is creating a culture of fear surrounding it. I worry that the specter of final judgment and the perceived smugness of "believers" can be terrifying to those who are seeking spiritual answers (before they realize there aren't any definitive ones). Believe what you believe. Just don't wield it like a weapon.

And remember I say all of this not as someone who is attempting to recruit Christians. I'm not. I am attempting to recruit thinkers; spiritual seekers; contemplators. I confess I know nothing of other religions' views of the ultimate ending, but I am troubled when Christianity's view of it becomes a defining characteristic. Too many doctrines seem to have been developed by the church to maintain its power and keep people afraid to turn away. Let's not, as individuals, perpetuate a practice of emphasizing fear over love, the real message of the Gospel.

Each of us knows his or her own brand of fear. It clouds our judgment and overwhelms other feelings and emotions. As such, I believe it has no place in spiritual exploration. I know that, for me, cancer has introduced into my life new categories of fear, but I am at my best when I can dispatch those fears with love, especially love of and for the people in my life—including the ones I have yet to meet. That is when I have a clear mind and spirit to take the next step in my spiritual journey, as well as my cancer journey. The former never ends and provides me with all I need to face the many endings of the latter.

It's the end of my world as I know it…and I feel fine.

Tastes Like Faith

March 31, 2014

Each time I receive an explanation packet for a new chemotherapy drug I look on the likely side effect list for one item: taste change. I have yet to see it. Maybe others have a different experience, but I think it's safe to say that the effects on a patient's taste buds are not high on the drug companies' lists of concerns. I mentioned this to my oncologist, and she agreed "they" generally don't note that as a problem. She also granted that she could see where this could have a real impact on quality of life.

Indeed. I will concede that among nausea, fatigue, hair loss, infection risk, etc., changes in taste may not rank at the top of one's list of concerns, but don't underestimate them. I like me some food. Without going into the details of the changes, I will just say that for a period of time after each treatment only certain foods with certain consistencies taste or even feel good in my mouth. And even after eating those foods I am left with an unpleasant aftertaste. Imagine a food you really don't care for. Now imagine taking a bite of that food every few minutes. It can dampen one's mood. Sometimes I can taste a food that I normally like very much, recognize a remnant of its original taste but can appreciate it not at all. It can turn something I love into something distasteful.

The good news is that my recent scan showed shrinking of my tumors on par with the response I had when I took these same drugs in 2012. After two failed efforts with other drugs, it's very good to be getting positive results and some payoff for all the unpleasantness, including an acute case of yuck mouth. More to the point: since the list of possible treatments after this is quite small, these results mean that my cancer journey continues a bit longer. And so does my spiritual journey.

Another way I hear people refer to this same journey is a "faith" journey, and I find myself struggling with this word. The dictionary tells us that "faith" means "confidence or trust in a person or thing," or, secondarily, "belief that is not based on proof." Not until you get to the third definition is there anything about God or religion, yet labels like "faith-based initiative" are often equated with religion. So is there more to faith than belief in a given religion?

Our understanding of the concept comes from all directions:

- "Now faith is the assurance of things hoped for, the conviction of things not seen."
  --*Hebrews 11:1 (NRSV)*
- **Luke Skywalker:** "I don't believe it."
  Yoda: "That...is why you fail."
  -- "The Empire Strikes Back"
- "Well I need someone to hold me, but I'll wait for somethin' more...I've got to have faith."
  -- George Michael

So, yes, the word can get diluted sometimes. But I submit that true faith is belief one holds very deeply. Yoda tells us it can move an X-wing fighter out of a swamp. The gospels have Jesus tell us it can move mountains and can even make you well. In fact, the Bible says Jesus' healing powers were limited in his home town due to the unbelief of the people. It's the disclaimer of every "faith" healer: if you are not healed you did not believe hard enough. Now, don't get me wrong; I am not equating Jesus with present day "healers," whether viewed by some as legitimate or not. My only point is that the onus is on you. How strong is your faith? And how far can that take you?

Inevitably when I engage people on questions of religion and spirituality we come to a point where there is no ready answer or clear proof for a given belief. Very often the next statement is something like, "That's where faith comes in." Some say it tentatively, as though it is something toward which they continue to strive. Others offer it as a badge of honor: whatever gaps remain in a rational explanation of religious beliefs are filled in by a steadfast faith—belief without proof. Either way, it’s true. At some point every belief system takes a leap of faith, including those that include no belief in any sort of God. Science alone cannot answer every question for us. Nor can the Bible. Nor the Quran. Nor any doctrine or treatise or story, taken alone or collectively. So what cannot be proven to us we fill in with faith.

And I do not hesitate to say that I have great respect for those who hold such a strong faith that they are willing to live it out. Whether it is a Mormon going on mission, a Jehovah's Witness sharing literature, a Baptist missionary headed to the third world or an atheist urging people to abandon religion altogether, I hold in high esteem anyone who is willing to act on his or her faith. I have had people tell me I have a strong faith. I'm not so sure. What I have is a healthy curiosity and a desire to explore the spiritual side of life, and I do this from a Christian perspective because that is my point of reference. But faith? Can one who is always questioning things also have faith?

This seems like a good opportunity to examine where, exactly, my faith lies. What are the things I believe strongly but for which I have no proof? I believe there is a God of some kind—some spiritual force of love and creation in the world that manifests in different ways for different people. I believe that how I treat the rest of creation, especially other people, is the most important element of my life and how I best stay connected to that God. And I believe there is more to life than my time here on earth—that my spirit will continue to exist in some way once my disease (or a runaway bus) ends my bodily existence. There are a number of other things I "think" and might even offer as "beliefs," but for right now—today—these are the ones that rise to the level of faith for me.

But here is the thing: I could be wrong. I am willing to

lead my life according to these faith principles, but even at this level I am unwilling to set them forth as absolute truths. How much more, then, should I be willing to maintain an open mind when dropping down a tier to discuss specific religious beliefs? People have argued that because I encourage others to question that I don't want them to hold any beliefs. On the contrary. Believe. Have faith. Sort out what that means for you and use it to guide how you live your life, and how you handle adversity, illness, death. But here is my entreaty to you: keep listening. Keep exploring. Keep thinking. Keep praying or talking or writing or drawing or gardening or whatever brings you closer to the spiritual side of life.

Too often when I hear someone say to me, "That's where faith comes in," I hear it as a closing door. This is where faith transforms into certainty, and the exploration ceases. Beyond the danger to ourselves of stunting spiritual growth, that closing door of certainty shuts us off from other people. We lose the benefit of their perspective and experience and erect barriers to spiritual connections. I would be greatly diminished if I lost some of the strong spiritual connections I have made with people whose belief systems look pretty different from my own.

When faith turns to certainty it loses its soothing flavor and becomes repellant. I can still recognize the remnant of faith that remains, but I cannot savor it. When the spiritual exploration ends, it leaves a bad taste in my mouth.

What Dya Tink I Said?

May 15, 2014

I had the good fortune recently to spend a week in Dublin (Ireland, not Ohio, though I've been there for work before, too; smells like Buckeyes. Ew). It was mostly long days at the office and nights working in the hotel, but I did set aside some time for sightseeing before I headed home. You don't need me to tell you it's beautiful country. Even if you haven't been there you've seen the pictures. What I didn't know but quickly learned about Ireland, though, is that there is a wide range of accents among the population. My Irish work colleagues I never even had to ask to repeat themselves. On the other hand, I mostly smiled and nodded at my taxi driver on the way in from the airport. I entered the country thinking I was going to need an interpreter for my own native tongue.

It was largely the same with my tour bus driver, Frankie (who I imagined was really Frankie the Fist or Frankie Two Toes, but then I've seen a lot of movies). Frankie is a second tier racist with basically a good heart and a fierce love for his mother and the Virgin Mary. In other words, he's Irish. Because I was the only one on the tour bus to Wicklow who was alone, Frankie chatted with me at every stop. As we stood alongside the bridge from the movie "P.S. I Love You," famous only in Ireland, Frankie began to rant—

somewhat anachronistically, I thought—about the "PC police." He explained, "If I call someone a 'black bastard' (blawk bawstud) it's just because he's black. If he was white I would call him a 'white bastard.'" I doubted this, and not just because 95 percent of Ireland is white, making Caucasian status a less than effective identifier. Here I felt like I needed a different sort of interpreter: less language and more cultural. Or maybe I understood exactly what he meant.

I returned home to get an updated CT scan, and once again interpretation was in order. I've seen my share of radiology reports, so it wasn't really a technical explanation I needed. It was more a case of me deciding how to process the results. It was good news, to be sure. The doctor came in with thumbs up, literally, and said that the tumors in my lungs continued to shrink since my previous scan; the only qualification was that the rate of shrinking is slowing. Now, I hate to be greedy, but this did temper my enthusiasm a little. See, it represents an inflection point in my journey. These chemotherapy drugs are the only ones that have been effective for me, and this result tells me that the clock has begun to run on their usefulness. They will be less and less effective until the disease mutates sufficiently that it overpowers the drugs. The likelihood of any other drug being nearly as effective is extremely low.

Of course, this is not news. I've known from the day I started chemotherapy that, even if I was lucky enough to get a good reaction, it would not last forever. Still, the reality of this inflection point forces me to decide how I am going to interpret what it means for me. At one extreme there is depression. If my mortality wasn't in my face enough, it certainly is now. I can project forward a couple of years and not much like the state of things. At the other extreme is jubilation. The vast majority of people don't get the kind of positive result I am getting from chemotherapy, and I can be thrilled at the additional time it has afforded me. But I have found peace by staying centered in between the extremes. Good news or bad, it is just the next thing, and I will take it as it comes. I am neither projecting out to the future nor putting too much stock in this recent result. It simply is. I appreciate each day no matter what the CT scan says.

I have taken a similar approach to my spiritual journey: listen, absorb, even devour…but do so without judgment or preconceived idea. Of course, I fail miserably; we all see the world through our frames, and I am no different. My upbringing, my education, my life experience, Star Wars, my family and friends—all these things and more influence how I see things and therefore how I process new ideas. Or old ideas, for that matter. In many ways it is easier for my liberal brain to accept a completely new idea than it is a traditional point of view. For example, if you ask me whether it is easier for me to accept that the apostle Paul's extensive writings on "fornication" are because he was a self-loathing homosexual or because there was so much aberrant sexual behavior going on in the places where he preached, I'm likely to say the former. But I fight against this. If I dismiss a more traditional point of view simply because it doesn't fit my frame, I limit my spiritual journey.

Shoot, even Paul used his own experience to interpret the gospel. Think everything in the Bible is the word of God? I respect that point of view, but my reading indicates that even Paul didn't think so. In I Corinthians 7:25 Paul writes, "Now concerning virgins, I have no command of the Lord, but I give my opinion as one who by the Lord's mercy is trustworthy." (NRSV) He prefaces statements elsewhere in a similar fashion. Now, you can say that God divinely inspired Paul to have the opinion that he did, but that's not what Paul says is happening. He is saying that he has been blessed by a nearness to God and so can be trusted to extrapolate the gospel to apply, in this case, to virginity. But it is still his interpretation.

I'm here to tell you I don't think there is a thing wrong with this. In fact, I don't believe it could be any other way. I am strangely comforted by the notion that the authors of the Bible were working through the meaning of what they saw and heard; every person in history before and after Jesus has been doing the same thing. Rather than deny it I think we should embrace it. Your life and loves and triumphs and failures have formed you into a unique human being with a unique perspective to lend to every idea and conversation and spiritual question. It is not better or worse than anyone else's—simply different. I invite you to own that while at the same time acknowledging the truth of it in others.

If I am perfectly honest, I will admit that my personal interpretations of my CT scan results are not always quite as centered as I would like. I get scared. But I strive for that peaceful place, and I allow others to help me. Perhaps that is all any of us who lacks the luck o' the Irish can expect of ourselves, no matter what each of us faces.

Holding Out For A Hero

June 9, 2014

As I emerge from this cycle of treatment I am feeling healthy and optimistic. The months immediately before me look to be more comfortable and full of fun and meaningful life experiences. And I will have hair for the summer. I hope each person who has encouraged me takes some satisfaction in the fact that I am entering a good period. Throughout my cancer journey I have been fortunate to have the support of a great many friends and family members. They demonstrate that support through prayer, but they also voice that support directly with encouraging texts, cards, emails, calls and through every other digital and analog medium imaginable. The messages are loving, thoughtful, even humorous...and at times misguided.

One of the themes of these messages is how brave people think I am for the way I am handling my disease. I have difficulty with this. I don't want to sound disingenuous. I recognize that I have found a peaceful place from which I begin each day and take each step on the path that cancer places in front of me. At times I have become aware that coming into contact with this peaceful approach is beneficial to others, whether they face cancer or some other challenge in their lives. I am grateful for that, and I hope I can maintain that peace and continue to share it. It's just that I don't think of it as bravery.

At the risk of over-simplifying, let me describe it this way: bravery is running into the burning building to rescue another person. I woke up in the burning building, and I'm just trying to keep the flames from consuming me. Now, there is something to be said for *the way* one goes about this, but who is to say one way is better than another? Some may turn inward, either in simple retreat from the world or to reach a new level of introspection. Some may take an aggressive stance, doing daily battle with the disease and living life with defiant vigor. All will experience fear at some level, but I don't know that bravery is how I would characterize the processing of that fear, no matter the method.

As unfair as the comparison is, my definition of bravery is grounded in my beliefs about my hero and standard for brave acts: Jesus of Nazareth. To make this case, though, I have to challenge a traditionally held belief (Hi, I'm Jason. This is what I do.). My assertion is that Jesus went forward with his ministry, calling out religious leaders and defying their extrapolations of Jewish law despite knowing for certain that doing so would lead to his death. This is different from the traditional notion that Jesus was sent here to die; that his death was inevitable. To me that traditional idea diminishes his life. If his suffering and death would occur no matter what he did, it required no bravery to conduct his ministry. The end would be the same, regardless, so he would simply do what good he could while he had time. But if Jesus of Nazareth had the choice of shrinking from his calling and saving his own life or embracing that calling and inviting tremendous suffering and death, can there be greater example of heroism in human history? If you consider yourself an atheist, non-religious or just non-Christian, is this still not a compelling reason to at least take a closer look at the gospel message?

I am not suggesting to Christians that they should abandon their belief that Jesus was sent to die for our sins simply because it makes him seem more heroic. But I can tell you I am much more impressed with a Jesus who *lived* for my sins, teaching love and compassion and starting a revolution that would cause the establishment to torture and kill him when they recognized that revolution taking root. This is the heart of why I call myself a Christian, and it's why I was so disappointed when my church recently began once again having us recite in worship the Apostles' Creed. I know this creed by heart from reciting it every week growing up, but as an adult I find it not only inadequate—I find it offensive. Even if I believed everything in it, from the virgin birth to the bodily resurrection to the second coming and judgment, I would still be frustrated by its complete omission of Jesus' life and ministry. I am not a Christian because Jesus was born, suffered, died and was resurrected. I am a Christian because Jesus cared for the marginalized, taught forgiveness and loved recklessly and passionately—all in the face of a suffering and death none of us today can comprehend. I will not recite a creed that supposedly defines my belief system when it ignores who Jesus was and what he did. To me this is the mother of all "yada yadas."

But let's go back to the idea of "how" and give it its due. If you accept my thesis, Jesus clearly ran into the burning building to rescue, well, everyone. EVERYONE. (Imagine me articulating this word like Gary Oldman's dirty cop in "The Professional" telling his subordinates whom to bring.) His message and example are there for all—regardless of religion or lack thereof—to use as a model for our lives. Once his fate was assured, though, and suffering and death were no longer an eventual certainty but an imminent threat and then a present reality, how Jesus responded was all the more impressive. They accused him and spat at him, and he responded with love and forgiveness. They tortured him and mocked him, and he responded with love and forgiveness. They put him to death, and...well, you get the pattern. Maybe this isn't bravery since he was already inside the building at this point, but it is no less valuable as an example for us (hopefully in much less extreme circumstances). The "how" does matter.

At the risk of stating the obvious, I think it's important who we set up as heroes, especially as we teach our children. Regardless of how I or anyone else handles a cancer diagnosis, I am not sure "brave" or "heroic" hits the mark. More commonly today we call our military "heroes," and I confess this worries me. There is no question what these men and women do is brave, as no one made them enlist and place their lives in danger. Hey, Iron Man wasn't considered a hero by Captain America until he flew into the wormhole at the risk of his own life, right? But despite my respect for and support of these soldiers (and superheroes) I wonder whether those associated with war should be identified as heroes so prominently in our culture. A hero is someone we want to emulate. I would rather we look to heroes of non-violence, love and compassion, with Jesus as the most poignant and perfect example.

So I may not consider myself brave, but that will not keep me from striving to be so in the example of Jesus. I can still charge into the burning building if I can find ways to take risks in order to care for others. It might be my comfort zone or my financial security or even my own safety. Where are the flames in your life? Don't "yada yada" the best part.

I Can Do Cancer All By Myself

June 30, 2014

We returned to our midtown Manhattan hotel last week, and my wife surprised me. It's nice when that can happen after nearly 16 years of marriage. What surprised me was that she hadn't really considered what we had just heard to be bad news. You see, I periodically consult with an oncologist at Memorial Sloan Kettering in NYC, and in this case the timing worked out that he was the one to reveal my latest scan results. It seems the shrinking that had slowed last time has now stopped. No growth, but no shrinking. The clock on my treatment's effectiveness continues to move.

As we waited for the tiny elevator up to our room in this old hotel, she considered my assertion that this was, at least, not good news. She wasn't being callous. She was being positive. And I commented on how symbiotic our relationship is with respect to my illness. We keep each other level and on a plane of peace, and there are times when I very much need that.

And though I am not one to see signs in everything, I couldn't help but be amused by the fact that the Priceline hotel I booked placed us right next door to the Eugene O'Neill theatre where "The Book of

Mormon" plays to sold out audiences. I took it as a wink from the Big Guy.

So this past week I began a course of chemotherapy that includes just one of the two drugs I have been taking this year—one that should be the easier of the two on me. Even so, this weekend has been no treat. It has me looking ahead and thinking about how I will increasingly need things done for me and how fortunate I am to have a wife and many others more than willing to help. But the truth is that I have spent much more time this weekend thinking of someone other than myself. I spoke this past week with a very good friend who is having his own health issues, including a cancer scare that is as yet unresolved. It is serious enough that he was talking in terms of how he does not fear death but fears more the burden he may be placing on his family. Everyone's experience with illness is different, but this I understood completely.

More than once I have commented to my family and to others that I would much rather take this on myself than to watch a loved one go through it. As a result I have an idea of what this illness does to my family. This isn't the reason I try to put the disease in a corner and take on the lion's share of responsibility for managing it—that's just in my DNA. But so is protecting my family. It's the same for my friend. We would each like to take on the entire burden and shield our loved ones from pain and loss and, ultimately, loneliness. But if I've learned anything during this journey it's that not only is that not possible—it's not even desirable.

Of course it would be ideal if the whole thing was taken away from us all. But once you accept the disease as reality, it's much better to share it. Those who love me want to help where they can. They're feeling pain anyway; if they can go through some of that with me instead of apart from me and even find ways to help me when I need it, then that is a gift to them. And so I fight the instinct to take it all on myself and sometimes have even allowed people to do things for me when I really haven't needed it. Too bad I couldn't figure out how to get people to do that before I was sick.

This desire to take on the entire burden for others sounds a little like a Jesus complex, though that's certainly not what I or my friend intends. Still, this idea lies at the heart of Christian theology for many. God sent his son to die as the perfect sacrifice, taking on all the sins of the world and redeeming them. To be honest this is something I took at face value growing up in the church, though it's something I never really understood. As I follow my spiritual journey it's something that makes less and less sense to me. How does this work? Why was this death necessary for God to forgive us? What does this mean for those who don't know Jesus or don't buy into the whole plan?

No matter whether you believe in the concept of Christ's sacrifice, it is a beautiful idea: the Son of God offered as the ultimate sacrifice to bear the sins of the entire world so that we are no longer saved by adherence to the Law but rather by grace. There is nothing we can do to earn salvation—it is a gift, a result of the sacrificial Lamb of God.

But do we sometimes see Jesus more as the scapegoat than the lamb?

There is a danger in heaping the entire burden onto Jesus: what is left for us to do? Certainly the bible doesn't stop at our forgiveness. There are a number of places where the apostles talk about the need to conduct ourselves in a way that is consistent with Jesus' message of love and compassion. The book of James is well known for its statement that faith without works is dead. Still, I think one of the things that turns some people off to Christianity is the way some Christians view it as a competition they've already won. "I believe in Jesus, and he died for my sins, so I am forgiven and saved." End of story. The final disposition of one's eternal soul is assured, so what is left to accomplish? How about creating the kingdom of God here on earth? Who's doing that, Bob the Builder?

Whether you believe in the sacrifice of Jesus or not, I submit to you that no religion or theology should thrive that takes all the responsibility out of our hands. Honestly, the older I get the less I care whether Jesus died for my sins or not. What matters to me is the message and example of love he brought and what it tells me about how I can contribute to the ongoing creation. That truly is something that is available to everyone as a free gift, regardless of where your spiritual journey takes you.

And it reinforces for me that in my own life and cancer journey I should not attempt to take on the entire burden myself. The same applies to all of us with whatever difficulties we face. Sharing the responsibility and allowing others to show us love is a blessing to them. We all wish we could spare our loved ones pain, but we cannot. What we can do is bring them into the experience and enable them to contribute to the ongoing creation that is each of us.

Balancing the Bucket

August 5, 2014

I do NOT want to think about money. I hate it. My family generally makes its career and other decisions on factors other than money, and of that I am proud. But who am I kidding? I have had the luxury of not thinking much about money because my parents gave me a college education. I started my career at a meager salary but did so debt free. From there I have had some good fortune and have been able to live simply and flexibly without having to think much about money.

Lately, however, thoughts of dollars and cents have been harshing my mellow.

Last month I had a bone scan, revealing tumors in my ribs and pelvis to go with the ones in my spine that we saw on previous scans. The doctor doesn't believe these are new. They likely formed at the same time as the spinal tumors—we just couldn't see them on the CTs or MRIs. However, this is combined with the fact that chemotherapy is becoming less effective as well as my inability to receive treatment the past two weeks due to unexplained low white blood cells, possibly due to the cumulative effects of chemo. The result is a feeling that the disease is beginning to get away from us. Ironically, I feel today nearly as good as I have in the past three-plus years. There is just this sense that I am standing on the edge of decline.

I expect it is this collection of facts that has had me thinking bucket list of late—quite unintentionally. It's not a sign I am ready to kick said bucket; it's just a reality. My mind goes to those things that I want to do before I leave this earth. Some of them are simply a matter of making time and/or developing the courage. Others require help from someone else. But some, not surprisingly, cost $$$. (And some take all three: I'm looking at you, stunt driving school) This is where I feel like I failed by not making a bucket list sooner—well before my diagnosis. Shouldn't we all be thinking about those things we most want to do, in part so that we can start planning and saving for them? Many of mine are travel-related, which is never cheap. And the fact that I didn't think about it before likely contributed to my wife and I weighting our savings heavily toward retirement. Yea. Can we all lobby our legislators for a "sucky diagnosis" exception to the 401(k) withdrawal penalty?

Some of you may enjoy thinking about money, but I expect most of us end up contemplating our finances a bit more than we'd like—it's not just cancer patients with high medical bills. It could be lack of employment or the rising cost of college for our kids (both of which are also affecting our family) or any number of things.

It's quite a luxury if you are only worried about how to pay for that hiking vacation in New Zealand.

Vacation, in fact, is one of the factors influencing my fiscal preoccupation of late. We recently returned from a trip to London (scratch driving in England off my bucket list—not even a ding on the car we "hired"), and the exchange rate with the British pound was staggering. But the money issue was also in my face with respect to the Church of England. A tour of St. Paul's Cathedral and a walk around Westminster Abbey—not to mention the religious elements of the Crown Jewels—left me contemplating just how much money Christianity has spent across two millennia in the name of luxury and beauty. And I've never even been to the Vatican. Is this how we have honored the gospel message? I can see why the guy in the Indiana Jones movie chose the wrong grail.

That's ancient history, though, right? Or it's just Catholics and Episcopalians. Or it's just the megachurches. Or it's just Christian churches. Or it's just... well, it's not me or my church, anyway. Really? How much of the money we contribute to our respective churches, synagogues, mosques, etc., goes to helping others, and how much goes to upkeep and beautification of a facility?

Look, I know this is a very old argument. Contemporary churches feel they have to have facilities in order to serve their congregations and have to be attractive in order to bring in new members. *Then* they can point those people back out into the community in service. And there is no denying the efficacy of organized religion in executing mission work. In fact, Catholics are probably the best example of this. I get it. But does anyone else have difficulty when your church spends tens of thousands of dollars on sanctuary modernization rather than seeding a new mission program? When it builds a huge facility for recreational activities and then refuses to use it to serve the community?

Ultimately, we're not going to solve the issue of church finances during our little online discussion here. There are well-meaning, faithful people on every side of it, and it's not simple. Still, I can't help but struggle with what place money has in spiritual exploration. I'm just more concerned with it at a personal level.

If the meaning of my life is to contribute to the ongoing creation, then how do I spend my money in service of that objective—especially now? Is it okay that I keep a job that does not directly benefit my fellow man or woman as long as I am taking care of my family? Is my house too big when the extra mortgage money every month could take someone else off the streets?

You can see where this goes. Pretty soon you're a less dramatic version of Oscar Schindler lamenting that if you switched brands of yogurt you could keep someone's kid in snow boots. We're all at different disposable income levels, and we're all at different places in our spiritual journeys. Each of us has to find the right balance. I still want to see Southeast Asia and South America and Eastern Europe and Africa before I die. I also want to become actively involved in charity work on a regular basis. I want to find more time to write. And I have no idea how to balance these things out.

My sister would tell me I'm a good person and that I shouldn't let money stress me out. I don't. But a little anxiety over how I spend my resources is healthy. Don't wait until your bucket list emerges to consider how to get the balance right.

Sick Like Me

August 18, 2014

I am continually struck by the number of people dealing with serious health issues at any one time. Whenever I go down to Washington University's Center for Advanced Medicine, as I did last week, it is always so busy. I recognize people come from far away to take advantage of Wash U's expertise, but it is still striking. I mean, these are just the people who are so messed up or have such complex or rare conditions that they need "advanced" medicine. It makes self-pity a bit challenging. I can still achieve it—I just have to work a little harder at it.

A more specific example: I am about to enter a clinical trial for a drug approved for renal cancer but not for head and neck, which is what I officially have. Prior to learning about this study I did a search on the government clinical trials website looking just for my cell type and came up with 250 studies. Of these I only appeared to qualify for two, and they were geographically nowhere near me. So it's a bit stunning that timing is so critical on the study I am about to start. That is, there are enough people relatively locally with a diagnosis and situation close enough to mine that they also qualify for this study that I could lose my spot if I did not decide to enter it right away.

We (cancer patients, membership credentials required) are told and often tell others that each cancer experience is unique. Drugs affect each person differently, our physical conditions otherwise are different, our diseases behave differently—and it's very true. However, we can sometimes forget how alone we are NOT, even in our fairly specific circumstances. We may not always find and interact with those people, but we should remember that they are out there.

More broadly, there are cancer stories everywhere. Today a black woman at my church came up to me and asked how I am doing. She mentioned how my hair is growing back in and related how she felt when her hair grew back after her own chemotherapy experience. I hate that almost everyone has a cancer story either about themselves or someone they love, but it can be helpful spiritually to share those stories with one another.

Now, why would I mention that she is black? Because I live in the FERGUSON-Florissant school district in Missouri, where we have been living together, white and black, for many years in peace. And my church is a rare example of white and black people worshipping together as part of a faith community. As much as media coverage may focus on our differences, I find myself thinking of our commonalities. As much as I embrace diversity and think we should celebrate and learn from how we are different, at times I think it is useful to remember how we are the same. As I look around the world, not just North St. Louis County, it feels like this is one of those times.

I have a theory: every bad thing that one does is a reflection of how one feels about oneself. This is the bully thesis: "He only picks on you to make himself feel better." (I'm not saying my mother ever had to say that to me. Not at all. It's not like I was puny or nerdy in school. It's not like I used to read comic books to imagine myself as powerful. Why are you looking at me like that?) As scary as bullies can be, what's truly frightening is that they grow up, often not feeling any better about themselves. What may be more frightening still is to think that perhaps each of us is or can be a bully to some extent. And it's grounded in this emphasis on our differences.

I am in no position to break down the intricacies of ethnic disputes, geopolitical disagreements or racial tensions. But I can hypothesize. There are reasons that poverty and oppression breed criminals and terrorists. But fear of those who are oppressed can breed bully behavior, as well—all in the name of making us feel better about ourselves. I'm afraid of you or I'm better than you or you deserve to be put down because you're Jew or Palestinian; because you're Ukrainian or Russian; because you're Sunni or Shia or Kurd; because you're black or white; because you're a Cubs fan (well, that last one might be justified).

Perhaps most unsettling is how prominently religion figures into the unrest around the world. We see it and denounce it, but we see ourselves as separate from it. Those are extremists or that's only in other parts of the world or Christians don't behave that way... But let's be careful. Whether you are raised with religious beliefs or come to them through an emotional transformation, you can become conditioned to feel very strongly that you have answers—*the* answers. You may not hate people who don't share your beliefs, but you think those people are wrong. I have a great deal of respect for those who feel this way explicitly and faithfully endeavor to convert people to save their souls. I mean, if you thought (and maybe you do) I was in danger of burning in hell for all eternity I hope you would at least mention it. But are those people also listening? Are they respecting the people they mean to save?

Let's not put this all on Mormons and missionaries and Jehovah's Witnesses, though. How much of the common Christian belief system is built on rules and requirements? We often go well beyond the commandments of loving God and loving one another, adding that you must also believe in the virgin birth and bodily resurrection and the Second Coming and Jesus preferred strawberry to vanilla and... Perhaps most restrictive is that you must believe Jesus is the only true path to God. Maybe that's right. But I invite you to look closely at yourself. Why is it important to you that others share your beliefs? Is it your certainty and concern for others? Or could part of it be, in fact, your *un*certainty in search of validation?

I think it's possible that we can only understand ourselves and our place in this world and in eternity in relation to other people. If everyone is kinda the same, then how do I separate myself out to feel better about who I am? I may not be as good as that guy, but at least I'm better than those people. I may not be headed for the penthouse in heaven, but at least I get to go there. If everyone is "saved" and headed for the pearly gates then I cannot understand my position in the spiritual stratification.

Atheists don't get off the hook here. Are you so certain that there is no divine presence in the world, no deity of any kind that possibly had a hand in creation of all that is around us? Perhaps Christians or those of other religions have turned you off with dogma, but perhaps you, too, have some insecurities about your beliefs and seek out only those who validate them.

Maybe it's worthwhile at this point in our world's struggles to take a moment to remember how similar we all are. Illness like cancer is a great equalizer, reminding us we are all fragile humans. But no matter what you face—family strife, addiction, financial woes—there are others who face the same thing, and many of them are people of other races, ethnicities, economic classes, etc. Similarly, no matter where you are on your spiritual journey there are people who are working through the same questions. It can be easy to focus on our differences and use a "bully pulpit" to try to bring people to our way of believing. I encourage you to think instead about how similar we are in our struggles, our questions and our humanity. Perhaps then we can learn from one another's differences rather than being threatened by them.

Oh, the Humanity

September 13, 2014

I used to be so low maintenance. Wash my face, brush my teeth, and I was off to bed. I recalled those times nostalgically last night as I readied my present self to retire. First I took an anti-nausea pill so I could get to sleep. Then I worked shea butter into my feet where the skin is cracking around the toes—another chemo side effect. I was careful around the big toe that lost its nail from the last chemo drugs. I applied vitamin E oil to the chemo rash on my face, then gingerly worked it through my thin hair and into my scalp, where the rash is actually painful. I brushed my teeth but slowly and, again, gingerly due to the sensitive tongue and gums I've developed with the study drug I'm taking. I put ointment in my eye to keep it moist through the night since it does not close all the way. I applied antiperspirant to my head to slow the sweating that happens when I eat. Then I climbed into bed and lay my head on my pillow, which I had to cover with a towel because of the oil.

On other nights my wife rubs my legs which often become sore when I exercise. Sometimes she rubs the oil into my scalp for me. Sometimes she rubs... Well, not everything she does for me involves rubbing, but the rubbing is verrrry gooood.

I don't list out the steps of my evening prep in order to garner your sympathy. If you know me at all you know that is not I. I list them simply to be authentic and open and to communicate how frail I can feel sometimes. How this disease brings me face to face with more than just my mortality. It brings me up close and personal with my humanity. When I feel weak, I feel human.

Two years ago, as I was in the midst of my second and, to this point, most difficult course of chemotherapy I did a 25-mile bike ride to raise money for cancer research. Last year I rode 50 miles four weeks after a mandated six weeks of inactivity while recovering from brain surgery, and just after starting chemotherapy again. In two weeks I will attempt that 50 mile ride once more. Raising the money for research is gratifying, but accomplishing the ride itself is actually the chief reason I do it. It's empowering. This year I set the goal of being in better shape for the ride, and I got there, losing 15 pounds during August through diet and exercise (though try impressing an oncologist with your weight loss). But then the new drugs started to pile up on me, and exercise has become increasingly difficult. My legs hurt every time I get on the elliptical or ride my bike, and I get out of breath very easily. But I still do it, almost every day. And I will accomplish the 50-mile ride, no matter how long it takes.

I don't tell you about my challenging workout regimen so that you will think me brave or give me a virtual pat on the back. If you know me at all you know that is not I. I tell you this to illustrate that strength comes in many forms, and that it, too, can be part of a cancer journey. Of any human journey. When I feel strong, I feel human.

I have discussed before how humanity gets a bad rap. We tend to define it by weakness, imperfection, even failure. There is no question that as we look around us and then at ourselves we see ample evidence for this viewpoint. But most of us are fortunate enough to see on a daily basis evidence of compassion, of achievement, of strength in other human beings, and I refuse to believe these are all exceptions; that somehow so many have found the wherewithal to overcome their very natures with such regularity. No, I believe these qualities we admire are also part of human nature. In fact, I believe the closer we move in this direction, the more human we are.

In some ways, this worldview has made it easier for me to come to terms with the idea of Jesus Christ as both fully human and fully God, the kind of thing that makes a confirmand's head spin. It's not so confounding if you don't think of humanity and divinity as so far apart. Certainly I make a distinction between the two, but I reject the idea that they are polar opposites. Personally, I love the idea that Jesus was "fully" human. That sets his example as the definition of what humans can be or at least aspire to approach. It's actually the fully God part where I struggle.

Here is where I throw Christians a curveball (that's a baseball reference for my non-American readers…though I guess it could be a cricket reference, too. I do not get that sport.). Consider, if you will, that perhaps Jesus was not divine at all. Perhaps we largely have John's gospel to thank for that Christology and that Jesus was a remarkable, charismatic and truly extraordinary human being. He was not *the* Son of God but *a* son of God. If all humans experience a degree of separation from god or the divine spirit or however each of us defines that presence that is greater than we, what if Jesus' true distinction was that he came closer to that god than anyone on record? It took Anakin Skywalker a podracer, a lightsaber, a tricked out TIE fighter, a pair of uncomfortably attracted twins, six movies and nearly 30 years to bring balance to The Force. All Jesus needed was three years and pair of sandals. But that doesn't necessarily make him God.

Now I'm sure I've made some former confirmands' heads spin. But I submit to you that these ways of looking at Jesus may not be as far apart as they seem. In the traditional view, Jesus is the divine Son of God, sent to earth to give God a face, to teach us God's desires for us and to be the ultimate example for us to follow (I am intentionally leaving off the sacrificial lamb and resurrection parts—those are other discussions). If you remove the "divine" from that description, is it really so different? If, rather than being sent from "above," Jesus was a human being who was able to narrow the divide with God more successfully than anyone, doesn't he still warrant our love, admiration and discipleship?

Of course none of us knows the actual truth, but I offer this idea as more than just a means by which I can jar your thinking. There is a beauty in Jesus' humanity that all of us, as humans, can share. Each of us, when we are at our best, can be the face of God for another human being—sometimes when that person is at his or her worst. Each of us can seek to draw closer to our definitions of God and recognize the qualities of Jesus in others. We can be examples to those who are separated from the divine presence in the world and help one another find our paths back.

Instead of waiting for a Second Coming we can effect a daily presence that is utterly human...and holy.

My Name is Lucious

October 21, 2014

I squat down at the side of Forest Park Parkway as it runs alongside the park. I don't kneel. I don't bend. I squat because it is the only position where my quads don't burn from the cramping. It's 85 degrees on a bright and still Sunday afternoon, and a mere five miles stand between me and the finish line of this 50-mile fundraising bike ride. I begin to think that at least a portion of the money raised for cancer research might best be spent on alleviating chemo side effects. The cure is still years away; I could use some love right now.

Five miles left. Out of 50. And it's not even just the distance. I have conquered the tough hills of Ladue Road and Conway Road.   I have endured the humiliation of grinding up those slopes at a pace so plodding and desperate that you could track the revolutions of my spokes with the naked eye. I have stretched and rested and hydrated, and now I am incapacitated with only the easiest fraction of the course left before me.

I lean forward and rest my hand on the stone wall that lines the street along this section of the parkway. Its rough, hard surface inspires me, and I bang my helmeted head against it in frustration. I bark obscenities at my legs for their betrayal as I begin to realize that this ride may now be more than grueling for me; it may be impossible. This goal was self-imposed, and no one will think less of me for falling short. Correction: no one *else* will think less of me. I do not expect my body to function much beyond the feeble pace I have set today, but I do expect it to function. I fight back the further humiliation of tears as exhaustion sets in, fueled by self-pity. I am tired. I'm tired of it hurting when I wash my face. I'm tired of food not tasting right—or at all. I'm tired of the lopsided, scarred, blemished face that mocks me in the mirror. I'm tired of being professionally unproductive. Despite the relatively light side effects of my current treatments I have never felt as acutely diminished as I do at this moment, teetering awkwardly by the side of the road.

I bang my head again, and a very recent memory is jarred loose.

It is just three days earlier and I am at Subway, eating lunch prior to going in for treatment. I have done a couple of calls in the morning—just enough to remind me how little I am getting done this year—and now I am alone, reading while I eat one of the two remaining subs that I can still taste. The book is engaging, but my attention is abruptly drawn to the gentleman who has just come through the door.

"How you doin' today?" he says loudly enough that I almost respond as though he is shouting across the room to me. I look up and see that he is addressing his "sandwich artist," a young woman who was friendly enough to me, if unenthusiastic about it. The man engages her in conversation, and in a matter of seconds the young woman brightens with a genuine smile. "My name is Lucious," he booms, and now I am engaged. I realize I have never met someone named Lucious, and for the first time I realize I have always wanted to. But his moniker is of much less interest to the Subway employees and patrons—four of whom are now lined up behind him—than is his attitude.

It doesn't take long to realize that Lucious has some form of mental disability. He is a short, slightly overweight man and of indeterminate age, but certainly older than his childlike speech implies. He moves awkwardly. His pants are too long, and his long-sleeve polo shirt is buttoned all the way up. He is accompanied by a young woman who stands quietly a couple of steps behind him, as though supporting him while encouraging his independence. She is smiling; she has experienced similar scenes before, probably even today.

Lucious and his companion get their sandwiches and make their way to a table next to my own. I hear the woman speak for the first time, and they begin to talk about their plans for the day. I know virtually nothing about such things, but I am guessing traumatic brain injury. Lucious is planning to build something, and the young lady reviews what materials she has and what they must seek out at Wal-Mart. There are socks to be purchased, a park to be visited…but distracted as I am from my book I lose track of their conversation. I am preoccupied by "My name is Lucious," this one sentence that so exemplifies the light that emanates from this guy. I mean, who introduces oneself to a fast food employee?

But he's a simpleton, right? If he understood more about the world… I take one step down this path and stop myself. It is too easy to be dismissive. A warm gesture toward another human being—a gesture powerful enough to have residual effects on those nearby—requires no explanation and certainly no apology. It is a gift, and it is given freely and gleefully by a man with diminished mental capacity, but not diminished humanity. I don't know what struggles Lucious has endured during his life or even during his day to this point. What I know is that he has chosen to be a blessing to those around him. I nod to him and smile as best I can as I pass him on my way out the door to treatment.

Now as I squat by the stone wall I give it one more slam of the helmet, but this one is to clear my head of any thoughts of surrender. It will be three more weeks before I learn that my current course of treatment—the one that is sapping my strength and cramping my legs—is actually shrinking my tumors. For now I know only that it is a fact of my life, but not the sole defining fact.

I stand carefully and begin to walk gingerly toward my patient and supportive teammates. As I move, the pain begins to dissipate and I regain full range of motion temporarily. I don't know exactly what the streets ahead will bring, but I know the pain will return worse than before. There will be both uphill and down, and recovery may take longer each time I am struck down. But I am not alone. I am NOT diminished.

And I will finish the ride.

Every Little Thing The Reflex Does...

November 17, 2014

If you've never been on chemotherapy (and I hope you haven't and never will be) you may not realize some of the stranger things it can do to a patient. I know I didn't before I started. I got most of my information on chemo side effects from the movies. In the past three-and-a-half years, though, I have accumulated far more knowledge and experience than I would have liked (although, viewed another way, all that unpleasant experience is, at least, experience, if you see what I mean).

During my chemo experience I have taken six different drugs, sometimes individually and sometimes in combination. Throughout these courses of therapy I have experienced all the standard side effects that are familiar to most: nausea, fatigue, loss of appetite, compromised immune system and hair loss. Actually, only one of the six drugs I've taken causes hair loss, and I have never actually thrown up as a direct result of treatment, as they control that pretty well with medication. So the experience is not always the way it gets depicted in the movies. And in the movies the actors get to keep their eyebrows. Not fair.

The list of *potential* side effects goes well beyond those with which the average layperson is familiar. When I start a new drug I get the literature on it with a list of "likely" side effects, which they define as occurring in more than 10% of patients. That's it. Just 10%. Each person will experience a different combination of these, so you don't know what to expect. There can be as many as twenty or more on the list, and a lot of them are just strange. You have probably heard about chemo making things taste different, and I've discussed taste changes before. But what about muscle cramping? Neuropathy? Overgrown eyelashes? I've had elevated blood pressure, blood clots, dehydration, a rash that looks like acne, dry and cracked skin and one drug even turned my eyebrows and what few whiskers I have completely white. There are probably a number of others I can't remember, but that's OK. When I can't remember, my body will.

A couple of years ago I started a high dose of a couple of drugs, and within a few days I developed very red, enflamed skin on the left side of my neck where I had received radiation the year before. They called it "radiation recall." And right now I have the acne-like rash that covers my entire face except for the lower part of my left cheek where I received radiation (there were times in high school where I would have considered such an extreme acne treatment, had it been available). That is the only portion of my face that is clear. That's the good side. The bad side is that rash affects my scalp most painfully on the scar above my ear where I had brain surgery. For better or for worse, my body remembers what's happened to it and responds to new stimuli the only way it knows how, like a reflex.

In how many other areas of my life have I done the same thing? While it's true I am a naturally questioning person, I have still had the tendency at times to judge a person or idea simply based on my own limited experience. I accept certain things to be true, and when new, inconsistent information is presented, I respond instinctively and become enflamed. Who among us isn't guilty of this?

Religion seems to me to be an area where this danger exists, perhaps more than in any other sphere of our lives. While the evolution and advancement of thought is lauded in most circles, within religion it can feel like sin. Clinging to traditional views is considered a virtue, regardless of what science and our own human experience teach us. Some religions and denominations are more open than others, but the danger (if you agree with me that's what it is) exists in most. The thing is, many of these beliefs are like muscle memory that cause us to respond out of reflex; we've held them so long and they exist so deeply within us that we don't even realize it.

For me one of the most vivid and volatile examples of this is Christianity's response to homosexuality. I realize it's even worse in some other religions, but Christianity is what I know and what is dominant in the U.S. I have my own theories, as I think I've mentioned, as to why this particular issue is such a hot button, but I'm not going into those here. And I'm not going to go through all the scientific and biblical analyses to try and convince you one way or the other. I simply want to suggest that many Christians have deeply held beliefs on this topic that are based on little else than the fact that they are deeply held.

A recent illustration: we addressed this issue in our Sunday school class as part of the study of a book on how to interpret the Bible. We had spent weeks talking about how we do not and should not simply accept everything within the Bible as the divinely inspired Word of God. We eat seafood without scales. We wear clothes made of mixed fabrics. We don't slaughter entire populations when they are living where we want to live. In short, we select which elements of the Bible should guide our lives, with the example of Jesus as the ultimate standard. When we got to homosexuality, though, some still viewed it as a sin. For others, homosexuality might be OK, but the line was drawn at gay marriage. Why is it wrong? "Because the Bible says so."

I felt like Wile E. Coyote after getting hit with the anvil, shaking my head noisily to regain my senses. Wait, didn't we just...? Weren't we saying that...? But it didn't matter. For many reasonable people, this is a belief so deeply held that they simply react, despite any new information.

I know it's obvious where I stand on this topic, but that argument isn't even my point. Even if you come to the conclusion that homosexuality is, indeed, a sin or that gay marriage is wrong, I am just encouraging you to do so thoughtfully and with your eyes wide open. It's a broader point, and it applies to a variety of issues. Where are your blind spots? What are the beliefs you hold so deeply that you haven't taken them out for examination, maybe ever? And why not? If the belief is built on a strong foundation, what threat does a little scrutiny pose?

If having cancer has done anything to/for me, it has humbled me, reminding me how little I know. The science of it, the unpredictability...it's all very intimidating. But in this way (and really *only* in this way) I am grateful for it. Over the years I have grown increasingly comfortable with not knowing answers and embracing mystery in my religious life, and that has helped me handle my disease emotionally and spiritually. Cancer has forced me to become more comfortable with mystery in my physical and intellectual life, and that is more difficult for me. I realize it's the other way around for some. But many things in our lives generate mystery; you don't have to get cancer to feel like your world is unpredictable. Whatever those things are in your life, good or bad, my suggestion is to allow them to take you down a peg or two. Challenge your way of thinking, even where you think no challenge could possibly be viable—*especially* there. You have nothing to lose but perhaps an exciting new view of the world to gain.

Socrates said, "The unexamined life is not worth living." Of course, he was probably a homo.

JC Speaks!

I decided it was about time I had a sit down conversation with JC (aka Jason's Cancer). It's been over three years, and it's time to break the silence.

ME: You know, it's hard to believe we've been together for this long and have never spoken.

JC: Well, I can tell you I appreciate the invite. I expect you have some questions for me, but there are a few things I'd like to get cleared up, too.

ME: I confess I hadn't thought of that. Would you like to start?

JC: Sure, I'll fire one off the top of my head. What is your beef with us?

ME: My "beef?"

JC: You clearly have something against me and my kind. We've had some good long peaceful stretches, but then you're coming at us with a laser or some kind of drug that wipes out a bunch of us at once. There have been a couple of times when I wasn't sure we were going to make it.

ME: Just so we're clear...when you say "we"...

JC: Your cancer cells!

ME: Forgive me, but it sounds as though you are surprised to learn that we might have an adversarial relationship.

JC: Why should we be adversaries? Wasn't it the best when we were at peace? You weren't sick, and we were multiplying, completely unencumbered.

ME: What do you mean I wasn't--

(I cut myself off as JC gets a wistful expression and stares off in the distance. It is almost heartbreaking.)

ME: I tell you what. I know I said you could go first, but do you mind if we come back to your question and do me for a bit?

JC: *(still a little wistful)* Your call. *(he sighs)*

ME: I have so many questions, but let's start with an easy one. What kind of cell were you before you became a cancer cell?

JC: Ah, that's a good one. I hate to be the rude guest, but I'm afraid I can't tell you. There's a code. It's part of the mystique of being Stage IV. If I was a Stage II or Stage III I could tell you. But as a Stage IV I am sworn to secrecy.

ME: If you were Stage II or III I wouldn't need to ask.

JC: Ironic, ain't it? *(With this he pulls something out of his pocket and starts turning it in his mouth)*

ME: Is that a cigar?!

JC: Relax. I'm not gonna light it. I just like the smell.

ME: Well, it's a little unnerving for me. Could you put it away, please?

(He complies, but he does so with a look I remember well from high school. There is nothing to prepare you for the knowledge that you are not as cool as your own cancer.)

ME: Listen, I'm sorry. Can I get you something to drink instead? I should have offered up front. What would you like?

JC: Ya got anything with Aspartame? I absolutely *thrive* on that shit.

(I freeze in front of my mini-fridge full of Diet Coke)

ME: Um, no. Sorry. How about some grape juice?

JC: I'll pass. Why don't you just ask me another question? Hopefully I can answer this one.

ME: OK, how about this: How did you get from my head and neck and lungs to my brain?

JC: Another good one. I can't take any credit for that. It was all this one kid—

ME: What do you mean, "kid?"

JC: I just mean he was young. He was a cell you had grown fairly recently before he became a cancer cell.

(JC looks at my midsection) Maybe he was a fat cell. Anyway, this kid comes up to the big barrier…

ME: The blood brain barrier.

JC: Sure, OK. So everyone else who had gone for it hadn't even come close. And this kid just bounded over the sonofabitch like it was nothing, rising up like Christian Bale. Damnest thing I ever saw.

ME: You saw that movie?

JC: Well, *you* saw that movie. *(I start to speak but he cuts me off)* And, no, that does not mean I was an eye cell. Doesn't work that way.

ME: Anyway. Very impressive. *(There is much less enthusiasm in my voice, but JC is undeterred in his)*

JC: I know, right? *(He just shakes his head in fond remembrance. Then all at once his expression turns dark)* And then you go and cut him and everyone else he created right out.

ME: *All* of them are gone?

JC: Near as I can tell. But I've been wrong before.

(There is a lull while we each wonder where this is going)

JC: I get the feeling that you're holding back what you really want to ask me.

ME: Could be.

JC: Well, we're not getting any younger.

(When I'm done cringing I take a deep breath and let it go)

ME: Why?

JC: Why what?

ME: Why are you here? Why do I have cancer?

JC: You've always had cancer.

ME: What?! What does that even mean?

JC: Look, I don't know how it works in other people, but for as long as I've been around I have been waiting to become a cancer cell. Always knew it was going to happen. Just had to do my thing, put in my time.

ME: You *wanted* to become a cancer cell?

JC: Of course! Strongest, fastest cells on the block. And we reproduce like nobody's business, if ya get my meaning. *(He actually winks)*

ME: That makes absolutely no sense.

JC: *(crestfallen)* Well, it sounds good.

ME: Just so I'm clear, you grew inside me as a...

JC: Nice try. I'm not telling.

ME: You grew inside me as a normal, healthy cell and from your first day you knew you were eventually going to become a cancer cell. And not only were you OK with this, you were excited about it, anxious to turn into cancer. That about it?

JC: Let me just say I take offense at the terms "normal" and "healthy" with regard to my former self. It implies I am neither anymore.

(We just look at each other for a few beats)

ME: I think now might be a good time to go back to your original question.

JC: Lay it on me. Why are you attacking us?

ME: I'm no expert, but here's my understanding: Whatever mystery cell you were before you became cancer, you performed a function in my body. Something that helped me do what I need to do. When you became cancer you stopped doing that thing, and your sole purpose became creating more cancer. Stop smiling, this is serious. Let's take a lung cell, for example. I need my lungs to breathe. If enough of my lung cells become cancer cells, then my lungs stop functioning and I die.

JC: What do you mean you die?

ME: I mean I die. That's the endgame here. I have surgeries and beat you back with drugs because if I allow you to take over my body those essential functions of mine won't have enough cells to operate them. I will die.

JC: But if you die...

(I wait while the realization washes over him)

ME: Any way I could encourage you to take one for the team? Maybe take a dive for the good of the larger operation?

JC: Given what you've just told me I'm going to decide not to be offended. But the answer is still no.

ME: Did you understand what I—

JC: I got it, I got it. *(a long sigh)* But I don't have any choice. I have one purpose, and I have to pursue it. That's all I know. That's all there is for me. And I can safely say you have succeeded in sucking a lot of the joy out of it.

ME: Likewise, my friend.

JC: I thought you hated me.

ME: I thought you hated me.

JC: Well, this is quite a cluster. *(I just nod slowly)* Where do we go from here?

ME: Back to the salt mines, I guess. I'd like to keep it civil like this, though. When we sat down I had hoped to learn whether I had done something to deserve a disease as terrible as cancer. Now I realize you don't even think of yourself as a disease, and you don't have anything against me personally.

JC: Not at all, man. You're a part of me. I'm a part of you. Wherever we may travel. Whatever we go through.

ME: Isn't that from "Thelma & Louise?"

JC: You loved that movie.

ME: Well, I guess it's appropriate. But I am not holding your hand.

ABOUT THE AUTHOR

Jason Hill grew up in a small town in southern Michigan and has lived his adult life in suburban St. Louis where he currently resides with his wife and daughter. Turn-ons include dark chocolate, "Star Wars" and open-mindedness. Turn-offs include winter, chemotherapy and the Ohio State Buckeyes. He is the author of two novels: *Mother's Day* and *Daughter of God*, both available soon on Amazon. Follow his blog at cancerandchrist.com.

Made in the USA
Lexington, KY
11 February 2015